Foreword

This Exam Preparation book is intended for those preparing for the GIAC Certified Forensics Analyst certification.

This book is not a replacement for completing the course. This is a study aid to assist those who have completed an accredited course and preparing for the exam.

Do not underestimate the value of your own notes and study aids. The more you have, the more prepared you will be.

While it is not possible to pre-empt every question and content that MAY be asked in the GCFA exam, this book covers the main concepts covered within the Computer Forensics discipline.

Due to licensing rights, we are unable to provide actual GIAC Exam. However, the study notes and sample exam questions in this book will allow you to more easily prepare for a GIAC exam.

Ivanka Menken

Executive Director

The Art of Service

Write a review to receive any *free* eBook from our Catalog - $99 Value!

If you recently bought this book we would love to hear from you! Benefit from receiving a free eBook from our catalog at http://www.emereo.org/ if you write a review on Amazon (or the online store where you purchased this book) about your last purchase!

How does it work?

To post a review on Amazon, just log in to your account and click on the Create your own review button (under Customer Reviews) of the relevant product page. You can find examples of product reviews in Amazon. If you purchased from another online store, simply follow their procedures.

What happens when I submit my review?

Once you have submitted your review, send us an email at review@emereo.org with the link to your review, and the eBook you would like as our thank you from http://www.emereo.org/. Pick any book you like from the catalog, up to $99 RRP. You will receive an email with your eBook as download link. It is that simple!

Contents

1   GIAC Certified Forensics Analyst

The GIAC Certified Forensics Analyst (GCFA) is designed for individuals working in information security, computer forensics, and incident response. The certification covers the skills required to collect and analyze data from Windows and Linux computer systems. With the certification, candidates have demonstrated the knowledge, skills, and ability to perform formal investigations of incidents and handling advanced incident handling scenarios, such as internal and external data breaches, persistent threats, and anti-forensic techniques.

The exam covers:

- Application Footprinting
- Automated GUI Based Forensic Toolkits
- Computer Forensics Core
- E.U. Laws
- Evidence Acquisition/Analysis/Preservation Laws
- Evidence Integrity
- File Name Layer
- File Sorting and Hash Comparisons
- File System and Data Layer Examination
- File System Essentials
- File System Timeline Analysis
- Forensic Evidence Acquisition Imaging
- Forensic Investigation
- Forensic Reports
- Key Forensic Acquisition/Analysis Concepts
- Key Forensic Analysis Methods
- Key Windows File System Analysis Concepts
- Linux File System Basics
- Metadata Layer Examination

- Data Presentation

- U.S. Laws

- Volatile Evidence Gathering and Analysis

- Investigative Process Laws

- Windows FAT File System Basics

- Windows Internal File Metadata

- Windows NTFS File System Basics

- Windows Registry Analysis

- Windows Response and Volatile Evidence Collection

2   Exam Specifics

GCFA Exams must be proctored and a partnership exists with KRYTERION. Location of test sites can be obtained at http://www.giac.org/proctor/kryterion.php. Tests are conducted at a testing center. Registering for the certification must be done first and the process can reviewed at http://www.giac.org/information/schedule_proctored_exam.pdf.

Specifics about the exam are:

- Exam Number :   GCFA

- Time Limit: 240 minutes

- # of Questions: 150

- Question Type: Multiple Choice

- Passing Score: 69.3%

2.1   Exam Prerequisites

There are no prerequisites for the GCFA exam. Training is available from SANS: Computer Forensic Investigation and Incident Response, FOR-508.

Renewal can be done every 4 years.

3 Forensic Essentials

3.1 SIFT Forensic Workstation

The SIFT Forensic Workstation can be used in either the Windows or Linux environments. Many investigators will use a Linux installation of the workstation to perform analysis of Windows-based systems because of the power provided by Linux. GUI systems like Windows do not require a core fundamental knowledge of the file system. As a result, Windows is not the best environment to examine systems forensically.

Performing SIFT Forensic Workstation functions in a Linux environment enables an investigator to analyze several file system formats, including:

- Windows: MSDOS, FAT, VFAT, NTFS

- Mac: HFS

- Solaris: UFS

- Linux: EXT2/3

All programs associated with the Forensic Workstation are installed into the following directories:

- /usr/local/bin (compiled programs)

- /usr/local/src (source files)

- /forensics (files for Autopsy Toolset)

- /images (images seized from compromised systems)

- /mnt/hack (mount points for file system images)

The programs installed include:

- Autopsy and PTK

- The Sleuth Kit

- Mac-Robber

- Foremost

- Static Binaries

- WireShark

- Other tools

3.2   Computer Forensics

Computer forensics is a process of gathering and analyzing data free from distortion or bias. This evidence gathering is performed with the intent to reconstruct the data and identify the course of events on a system. The scope of forensics includes:

- Incident response

- Evidence acquisition

- Investigation and analysis

- Reporting results

Evidence is typically acquired during an incident response. This confirms the presence of an incident. Both volatile and non-volatile data is collected. Volatile data can be lost if the system is changed prior to the data being collected, therefore it ideal to collect the data before any action is taken to respond to the incident - even when the response is made by automated systems. Non-volatile data is found in memory disks (hard drives) that are powered off or static. The investigator will take the data and analyze it for the purpose of creating a clear understanding of the incident. Once that understanding is complete, the investigator will report all findings.

When gathering evidence, the order which the evidence is collected is critical since the efforts to obtain evidence from one source may change the evidence available at another. The system memory is the most volatile of all possible evidence, followed by network connections. The state of the system can be reconstructed by knowing the processes running on the system. If at any point the system is shut down, all the above information will be destroyed. Also volatile is the hard drive which is cleaned of temporary files when the system is powered down. The least volatile of all data exist on removable media, such as floppy disks or CDs. The following order should be used to gather evidence:

- Gather information on network connections

- Disconnect the system from the network

- Gather all volatile data available

- Verify the incident using logs, IDS, interviews, and system logs

- Gather images of the evidence

13

Typically, a response to an incident will find either a dead system or a live system. If the system is dead, all the volatile information will have been lost or the system will be left in the state in which it died. A dead system can be the result of disrupted power, the system being turned off, or an error in memory systems causing the system to crash. If the system is live, the first question that the investigator must ask is if the system has been restarted or rebooted between the time of the incident start and the point evidence is collected. If this is case, the volatile memory at the point of the incident may be gone. With live systems, evidence may be gathered over time using monitoring techniques - essentially creating a wiretap on the system.

From a forensic perspective, incident response will initially focus on verifying the existence of an incident. Eventually, response will focus on preventing further damage - especially evidence. Between verifying the incident's evidence and taking action to handle the incident, the focus in on gathering evidence. Techniques for evidence gathering concentrate on:

- Minimizing loss of data and evidence

- Avoiding data changes to the system

- Recovering service and data

- Minimizing downtime

In addition to investigative incident handling, media analysis generates a report identifying the source of the incident. It performs a static analysis of a copy of all evidence from the investigation, not the actual evidence in order to preserve the evidence for future analysis or collaboration. Many tools and techniques are used to analyze the data without changing the evidence. Media analysis is used to find specific data related to the crime behind the incident.

Evidence is used to establish or disprove a fact. The smallest piece of evidence usable in computer forensics is 4 bytes, which represents two octets of an IP address. The integrity of the evidence must be maintained throughout the analysis process: that is, the evidence cannot be altered in any way. For the actual analysis, bit-image copies of the evidence, or disk images, are used. The original evidence and pertinent findings are locked away with limited access granted. Cryptographic hash functions are used to ensure the integrity of original evidence and copies of that evidence. The integrity of the evidence will ensure that proper prosecution of responsible parties behind the incident.

As the investigation proceeds, clues will be found that provide more information to be obtained. In electronic forensics, key words specific to the case may be revealed. A list of these key words should be created for each case being investigated. This list is used to perform low level searches on the hard drive or other media. The list will be modified throughout the investigation and is primarily used to find key information in the evidence.

Disk images are a copy of the original evidence, specifically the original media used in media analysis. The disk image is collected by a tool by performing bit-level copying from one location to another location. Depending on the investigating case, several disk images may be obtained since they represent a system at a particular point in time. By comparing several disk images from the same system, it is possible to see the state and changes to the system as a result of the incident.

An investigator will perform forensic duties guided by four essential principles:

- Minimize data loss

- Right down everything

- Analyze all collected data

- Report findings

3.3   Security Threats

Any threat against the confidentiality, integrity, and availability of enterprise assets is a threat to be investigated. Recognized threats consist of:

- Denial of service

- Buffer overflows

- Mobile code

- Malicious software

- Password cracker

- Spoofing/masquerading

- Sniffers

- Eavesdropping

- Emanations

- Shoulder surfing

- Tapping

- Object reuse

- Data remnants

- Unauthorized targeted data mining

- Dumpster diving

- Backdoor/trapdoor

- Theft

- Intruders

- Social engineering

3.3.1 Denial of Service (DoS)

Denial of service attacks consist of:

- Consuming specific resources.

- System services or applications becoming unusable by users.

- Total failure of a system.

In the early 1990s, the most prevalent attacks were SYN attacks; TCP/IP protocol manipulation caused when an overwhelming number of open-ended session requests would be sent to a service, causing the service to focus on processing these requests while delaying legitimate requests. The result was that systems were virtually unusable by valid users and applications of the service.

Denial of service is typically a result of finding a weakness in system services and exploiting that weakness. One of the most common characteristic of a DoS attack is the use of multiple events, systems, or users to focus legitimate actions against a single system. The result is a manipulation of system interactions for the purpose of acquiring access or redirect communications.

3.3.2 Buffer Overflows

A portion of memory is usually allocated to temporarily store information that is used for processing. This is called a buffer and is essential to manage data input and outputs during system interaction.

A buffer overflow is a manipulation of the system's ability to manage the buffer which, in turn, causes a system failure such as an outage, failure to control the application state, or failure to control the data required for processing.

Poor system memory access control and management is the typical cause of buffer overflows. Proper coding of the application, services, and operating systems managing the memory allocation is a good start at preventing this threat. Adequate testing in the development process can ensure that the coding is done properly and identify any vulnerability to buffer overflows.

3.3.3 Mobile Code

Any software that is transmitted across a network from a remote source to a local system and executed without any explicit action from the user is referred to as mobile code. The local system can be a personal computer, smart device, PDA, mobile phone, or Internet appliance. Mobile code does not need to be installed or executed by the user and is typically known as downloadable code and active content.

Mobile code is not necessarily harmful and includes:

- ActiveX controls

- Java applets

- Browser scripts

- HTML e-mail

However, significant security implications surround mobile code because of the capabilities of dynamic distribution, limited user awareness, and potential for harm. Mobile code used maliciously can track user activity, access vital information or install other applications without the user's knowledge. To prevent malicious mobile code, the system has to be configured properly.

3.3.4 Malicious Software

Malicious software used to describe Trojans or spyware, but has expanded to include any software, application, applet, script, or digital material run on a computer system that can be a threat to the system, applications, or information.

Falling into the category of malicious software, or malware, are:

- Viruses – parasitic code which requires human assistance to transfer or insert into the system or is attached to another program to allow replication and distribution.

- Worms – self-propagating code which exploit vulnerabilities in systems or applications. Similar to viruses without the need for human interaction.

- Trojan Horses – any program that appears to the user as desirable but are, in the end, harmful.

- Spyware – hidden applications intended to track user's activity, obtain personal data, and even monitor system inputs.

3.3.5 Password Crackers

Passwords are a grouping of secret characters used to prove the identity of the user. Passwords are prone to discovery and given that they range from an average or 5 to 15 characters, they are limited by the number of potential combinations of characters.

Passwords are stored by a one-way hash, an algorithm producing a unique representation of the password. When a system receives a hashed password, it uses the same algorithm used to create the password and compares it the hash on file. If the hash is correct, the certainty that the password provided is on file increases. In most cases, the password is never stored or saved, only the hash.

Password crackers work on the hashed password which has been saved. When the file containing the hashed password is found, the password cracker compares every possible password combination against the hash. This is done by using or creating a list of possible combinations, hash them, and compare the hash to stored password on the file. The length and complexity of the password has an impact on the time required to test every combination, ranging from minutes to years.

Password crackers are easily obtainable and are useful for both hackers and system administrators. System administrators use password crackers to identify the strength of a particular password. If the password is weak, a request can be made to the user to change to a stronger password.

In 1980, Martin Hellman described a method of using precalculated data stored in memory to reduce the time required for cryptanalysis. By performing an exhaustive search and loading results into memory, time required to create a list for use by password crackers can be significantly decreased. This is commonly referred to as a time-memory tradeoff where saving memory and the cost of processing time compete with each other.

Many password hashes are generated by encrypting a fixed plaintext with the user's password as the key. A poorly designed password hashing scheme will result in the plaintext and encryption method being the same for all passwords. This allows password hashes to be calculated in advance and subjecting them to a time-memory tradeoff.

The Hellman concept is based on enciphering the plaintext with all possible keys whose results are organized into chains. Only the first and last elements are loaded into memory. As the number of stored chains increased, so did the frequency of generating the same results with different keys.

By 1982, Ron Rivest had introduced the concept of distinguishing points which improved simple password hashes by reducing the number of memory lookups. The distinguishing points were defined at the ends of the chains based on the fact that the first ten bits of the key were all zeros. When a plausible match is identified, a chain is pulled from memory from the end. Focus on the distinguishing points at the end reduced the time required to process passwords.

A faster time-memory trade-off was developed by Philippe Oechslin in 2003. The issue with the chaining process was the possibility of collision between chains and eventual mergers within memory. To limit the collision rates and reduce memory requirements, Oechslin proposed an approach to the creation of chains. His new chain structure was called rainbow chains and utilized the distinguished point concept with a process for successive reduction of points.

3.3.6 Spoofing/Masquerading

An attack method utilizing weaknesses with Internet protocols to gain access to systems based on IP addresses and inherent trust relationships were first conceived by Steve Bellovin. But Kevin Mitnick popularized the concept of IP spoofing in the 1980s. IP spoofing allows a person to appear to come from a trusted source when they are actually outside of the trusted environment.

Earlier versions of spoofing were performed at the protocol layer by sending packets to the server with the source address of a known system in the packet header. Filtering devices would pass the packet if they were configured to permit activity to and from the trusted address or network. Though this would allow the packet to arrive, it did not guarantee the desired response from the server.

Modern systems and firewalls compensate for spoofing attacks. Similar attacks manipulating the trust of systems and users are still prevalent. Phishing is another form of masquerading as a trusted source. Domain Name Servers can be used to redirect Internet users from valid websites to malicious sites. Spoofing is used in man-in-the-middle attacks where users may believe they are interacting with a desired destination when in fact they have been redirected through an intermediary who is collecting information from both sides of the communication.

Spoofing or masquerading has significant impact on the access control environment since attackers gain access in such a way that circumvents the established controls.

3.3.7 Sniffers, Eavesdropping, and Tapping

At some point in networking between to computers, communications will pass through a physical device. Gaining access to the physical device could provide insight into all layers of communication, in the form of eavesdropping or tapping.

The same capabilities are utilized by IDSs which monitor communications in an effort to detect unwanted activities.

Sniffers are devices collecting information from a communication medium.

3.3.8 Emanations

Emanation is a proliferation or propagation of a signal which is most evident in wireless networks. By being within range of the wireless signal, an attacker can attempt to access the network without physically accessing the facility.

Emanations can be tapped to allow eavesdropping. The key is tapping into the electromagnetic properties of computing devices to acquire data from a distance.

Encryption of signals can provide some protection. Reducing the emanation of a signal can also provide some protection using mechanisms such as TEMPEST.

3.3.9 Shoulder Surfing

Shoulder surfing is a form of social engineering where information is gathered through direct observation. Watching a person enter a password or listening to a conversation containing sensitive information.

Deterrents to shoulder surfing include:

- Awareness training

- One-time use passwords

- Multifactor authentication

- Screen filters

- Special polarized glasses

3.3.10   Object Reuse

The allocation or reallocation of system resources to an application or process is referred to as object reuse. In essence, applications and services create objects which are stored in memory. Those objects can be used over and over by the application or service and are shared with other applications and services. A object used to perform a privileged task for an application or authorized user. If the usage of this object is not controlled and remains in memory, it can become available to unauthorized use.

Application object reuse has two aspects:

- The direct employment of the object.

- The use of input or output data from the object.

To protect against the harmful reuse of an entire object, an application should erase all residual data from the object before it is assigned to another process to prevent the the data from being intentionally or unintentionally read.

Security requires a controlled sharing of object resources. Since these resources are in memory, their management can be difficult. Many systems are running multiple processes simultaneously. Memory may be allocated to one process for a while, deallocated and reallocated to another process making the constant processing of potential security vulnerability. This is because residual information may still exist in a memory section when it is reallocated to a new process.

The same concern is applicable to system media like hard drives, magnetic media, and other forms of data storage. It is common practice to reuse media to reduce costs in backup activities. Removing all data from the media ensures that proprietary and confidential information is compromised. Standard methods include:

- Degaussing

- Writing over media

3.3.11   Data Remanence

Similar to object reuse is data remanence which is often seen when used computer equipment is reused or sold to another user. The partial or entire remains of digital information still exist for the new user.

Hard drives are comprised of platters organized into segments and clusters. When files are written to the hard drive, it is placed in one or more clusters in a series or spread across the disk. The file allocation table is responsible for tracking the physical location information for the file in order to retrieve it later.

Several situations can lead to data exposure:

- Deleting a file removes the information from the file allocation table but not from the physical cluster.

- Sensitive or confidential data is stored in the slack space of partially used clusters and remains until the entire cluster is overwritten with new data.

- Malicious information or code is stored by attackers within the slack space.

The most effective mechanism to destroy data is to overwrite the data several times accomplishing:

- Providing enough randomization to prevent statistical analysis of the data.

- Further masking the remnants of any electromagnetic representation of the data with each rewrite.

3.3.12   Unauthorized Targeted Data Mining

Any collection of large amounts of information for the purpose of creating predictions is considered data mining. There are several reasons for data mining information and is often used to provide a logical determination about the information over specific data.

Hackers generally perform reconnaissance in order to collect as much information as possible to determine the operations, practices, technical architecture, and business cycles. Though individual pieces of data may be harmless, different combinations of data could be created and analyzed to identify vulnerabilities that can be exploited.

One common area of concern is marketing; where security is concerned that public information that is placed on web sites cannot be used against the company. In the early days of the Internet, a large amount of data was posted by companies to the Internet that aided hackers in determining how and what to attack. Current awareness ensures that sensitive information is not posted as easily, however the evolution of search engines has made finding sensitive information easier to discover.

3.3.13   Dumpster Diving

Dumpster diving is a simple tactic of rooting through trash to obtain enough information to make conclusion and create a strategy for attacking a target. The process is similar to data mining in stringing together small data of insignificant data together to obtain a large more harmful fact about the target.

Destroying documentation is one of the best chances against this vulnerability, as well as destruction of media to prevent exposure.

3.3.14   Backdoors and Trapdoors

Many creators of applications create special access capabilities into their software code for troubleshooting purposes. These created capabilities are commonly referred to as backdoors. If a person knows the location of the backdoor, then they can obtain access to the application or system without the knowledge of the system owner.

System Integrators create special rules and credentials to ensure they have complete access to the systems installed for the purpose of supporting their customer. Typically, the same methods and credentials are used for multiple customers. If a person was to obtain this information, they would have complete access over several customers' systems.

3.3.15   Theft

Physical theft is any item of value that an authorized person can remove. Digital theft does not require removal, but simply needs to be copied by an unauthorized person.

3.3.16   Social Engineering

Social Engineering is the use of coercion or misdirection to obtain information. It always consists of a degree of interaction, though that interaction may be on the telephone, through e-mail, or face-to-face.

E-mail social engineering is a common effort to use e-mail to obtain information. In most cases, an e-mail is sent disguised as coming from a trusted source. The message is a request for information. The victim believes they are sending the information to a source that has the right to know the information.

Help Desk fraud occurs when an attacker poised as an employee and calls the Help Desk for help. The goal of the attack was usually to reset a password. In some cases, remote-access phone numbers or IP addresses can be obtained. Attackers will sometimes poise as managers to obtain special privileges.

3.4   Methodology of Forensics

The Forensic Investigation Methodology consists of eight major steps:

- Verification

- System Description

- Evidence Acquisition

- Timeline Analysis

- Media Analysis

- String or Byte Search

- Data Recovery

- Results Reporting

This methodology can be used across any operating system, supported by any forensic tool, and should remain consistent from case to case. The first three steps are all part of Incident Response and Evidence Acquisition. The fourth through seventh steps are specific steps within Investigation and Analysis.

The verification step ensures that an incident has occurred. After verification, a system description is created for the system being analyzed. The questions that must be answered in the description are:

- Where was the system acquired?

- What was/is the system used for?

- What is the system's configuration?

- Any additional information pertinent to the investigation.

How the investigation is executed is affected by the system description. If the systems are critical to business operations, its operation may restrict the ability to shut down the system. A server will be handled differently than a workstation. How evidence is acquired will be determined by the function and criticality of the system.

Media analysis will examine an image using any forensic tool. The analysis systems used should be described in detail, as well as the tools used. Some tools will have multiple functions which may or may not be used. How the tool is used should be documented, specifically noting how the tools did not modify the evidence when performing the examination.

When performing the media analysis, many different tasks will be performed. A few of those tasks are:

- Check the file system for modifications to the operating system software or configuration.

- Check the file system for any back doors, setuid files or setgid files.

- Check the file system for evidence of a sniffer program.

- Check all history files, especially for the Internet.

- Check the system registry or /proc.

- Check start-up files and processes.

String and Byte searches are used to find data on the collected evidence. Everything should be searched: unallocated space, allocated space, and file slack. The tools used should be able to tell the investigator the location of all search hits to allow examination of the information surrounding the file.

When recovering data, the focus should be on recovering the files or data which have been deleted or in slack from the system. To do this successfully, the affected files must be identified first. The most pertinent files should be recovered first. The methods for recovering the data should be described in detail in the written report.

The report must include all information pertinent to the investigation. Ultimately, the report will either support any assertions about the incident or reject the assertions about the incident. The final report should be detailed and clear enough to allow for submission in potential court cases. When taken to court, the finding must be able stand against opposing questions from representatives of the court.

3.5   File System Basics

Numbers are generally represented in three ways: as a decimal, a hexadecimal, or binary. Decimal representations are mathematically base 10 numbers. That is, numbers are represented by 10 different digits and new sets are started after every 10 counts. The digits used are 0-9. Hexadecimal representations are base 16 numbers, using the numerical digits 0-9 and alphabetic digits A-F (or a-f). Binary representations are base 2 and use either a 1 or 0.

Given these methods, the same number can be represented differently. For instance, the number 35 in each of the forms are:

- Decimal = 35

- Hexadecimal = 23

- Binary = 00100011

The decimal version is easy for most people since this is how most mathematical systems in business are based. Since hexadecimal is based 16, 16 goes into 35 twice with 3 left over (35-16-16=2). Therefore the first digit represents 16x2, while the second digit is the remainder. Each hexadecimal notation has two digits with the greatest number being 256 (16x16). The binary representation is consistent with bits and bytes structure. A single byte consists of 8 bits and in computer language represented by 8 positions. Each position represents a different value from right to left - all adding to 255:

1	1	1	1	1	1	1	1
128	64	32	16	8	4	2	1

The binary representation of 35 is understood because of the one in the 3rd, 7th, and 8th position of the binary representation - 32+2+1 = 35. The most recognized computer concept using binary systems in the IPv4 address.

Here's another example using 158:

- Decimal = 158

- Hexadecimal = 9D (9x16 + 14 or 9X16 + D)

- Binary = 10010100 (128+16+4)

Obviously, hexadecimal and binary representations can seem limiting because of how they are written, specifically with decimal numbers greater than 255. IP addresses are a perfect example of this dilemma. If a person need to support 1000 IP addresses, multi-byte data types would be useful. Here's how they would look respectively from 1 to 1000:

- Decimal = 1 to 1000

- Hexadecimal = 00 00 to 03 D8

- Binary = 00000000.00000001 to 00000011.00010101

Given the decimal point, what is being shown is 3x255 (or 256) + 24 (or 21). In reality, the decimal representation is normally written as 0.1 to 3.235. This is of course a generalized explanation of how numbers work in computers. Numbers can be displayed differently to how they are written: either big-endian or little-endian. Big-endian will store the most significant byte is stored at the lowest address - Byte0 Byte1 Byte2 Byte3. Mainframe systems store bytes in this manner. Therefore, the hex number 'af be 02 45' is stored as 'af be 02 45'. Little-endian is seen in Intel based systems. The most significant byte is stored at the highest address - Byte2 Byte2 Byte1 Byte0. The same hex number 'af be 02 45' is stored as '45 02 be af'. This difference poses a problem when converting numbers between two systems: the problem is commonly called the NUXI problem, because Big-Endian systems would store UNIX as UNIX, but as NUXI in little-endian systems.

3.5.1 Partitions

All x86-based systems will use DOS-based partitions. The first sector of a disk will contain a partition table describing 4 partitions. The partition table has information about where the partition will start, end, and what type of partition it is. A Cylinder Head Sector (CHS) address is also present for all partitions, but cannot describe the size of full disks. The addresses are in the first 512-byte sector and contained in the Master Boot Record. Entries are in specific points of the 512 byte sector:

- First Partition - byte 446 (offset 0x1BE)

- Second Partition - byte 462 (offset 0x1CE)

- Third Partition - byte 478 (offset 0x1DE)

- Fourth Partition - byte 494 (offset 0x1EE)

Every partition table will always end with the value 0x55 and 0xAA.

Each entry in the partition table is exactly 16 bytes long and defines the type of partition, the length, starting location and physical parameters of the hard drive. The content of the partition entry are described below (Offset, Length, and Content):

0	1	State of partition: 80h if active, else 00h
1	1	Start of partition (Head)
2	2	Start of partition (Sector and cylinder)
4	1	Type of partition
5	1	End of partition (Head)
6	2	End of partition (Sector and cylinder)
8	4	Distance from partition table to first sector
12	4	Number of sectors in the partition

The three primary areas used by forensic tools are the partition type, logical start of the partition, and the length of partitions in sectors. The common types of partitions are (with their hex value):

FAT12	0x01
FAT16	0x0E
FAT32	0x0C
Linux Native	0x83
Linux Swap	0x82
BSD/386	0xA5
Extended	0x05
NTFS	0x07

The maximum partition size for a MBR DOS-based partition is 2 TeraBytes.

In modern computing, a partition table with four entries is very limiting. Extended partitions can be used to exceed this limit. An extended partition will contain another partition table and two more partitions. One of the additional partitions can contain a file system and the other partition can be another extended partition. Extended partitions can be created inside each other until all the disk space is used. Usually, only the file system partitions need to be extracted.

3.5.2 Data Storage

Bytes of data are stored on the data layer. Data layers are part of a file system. Sectors in a file system are units of data, typically 512-bytes in size. Files can be allocated in consecutive sectors, allowing larger data units to be stored. The size of a data unit can range from 1 sector to 32 sectors (or more).

The different file systems will call data units by different names:

- FAT: clusters

- NTFS: clusters

- FFS: blocks

- EXT2FS: blocks

28

A file system is comprised of five layers:

- Physical - the physical drive

- File System - information about the partition

- Data - clusters or blocks

- Metadata - information on structure

- File Name - name of the file

Besides the Data Layer, the File System layer is very important. This layer contains the information related to the file system structure, such as data unit sizes, structure offsets, and mounting information. Users can configure the file system to meet their needs. These configurations are found on the File System Layer and later used to mount the partition by the operating system.

Data is either allocation of unallocated. Allocated data describes clusters or blocks which are being used by an existing file on the system. Unallocated data refers to clusters or blocks which are waiting to be used. Sometimes called free space, unallocated data could represent where files existed but were deleted. Though space is unallocated, evidence can still be recovered even when common file recovery tools cannot recover the data. This is because a file fragment, or piece of the file, may be present. A file fragment may be one or more blocks of data which, by itself, cannot contain a full file.

To understand how pieces of files can be recoverable even when deleted from the system, it is important to understand how data is written to the disk. Consider writing data in a contiguous manner: that is the first block is used, then the next, and the next, until all the disk space is used. Let's say two files taking up 30 blocks of space are safe. Initially, the first file will consume the first 30 blocks, and the second file will consume the next. Now, the first file is modified and 5 additional blocks are required. Since, the next 5 blocks are already being used by the second file, the entire 35 blocks of data must be rewritten after the second file: therefore taking up blocks 61-95. The first thirty blocks are now free (unallocated); however, the original file still exists in those blocks.

If a third file is saved to the disk which requires less than 30 blocks of space, it could be written within this first 30 blocks. If this first file requires 20 blocks, 10 blocks of the original first file will still be on the disk until written over. Most file systems will try to save data in contiguous blocks or clusters. However, if the file is too large to fit into contiguous blocks or clusters, the file systems will deliberately fragment the file.

Windows file systems use fixed-size clusters, typically 2048 bytes long or four sectors. If the actual data stored is less than the available cluster space, the entire cluster is reserved. The system will write data to the disk in sector-sized blocks. If a file is 1350 bytes, it will be written to the first three sectors of the cluster. The file will completely fill two sectors and partially fill the third. The remainder of the third sector will use null bytes to fill the remainder of the sector. Since the entire cluster is reserved and the fourth sector is not used, this extra space is considered slack space.

Unix file systems also has slack space but it is overwritten to the end of the block with the null byte. Data found in slack space is rare, but can be written using data hiding tools, such as BMAP.

3.5.3 Metadata Layer

The Metadata Layer points to the Data Layer, providing cataloging capabilities. In this layer, the operating system is told which blocks or clusters are assigned to the file represented by the layer. The layer is comprised of inodes: which are identified by an inode number, name, type, permissions, and size. Each inode will assign MAC times and represents a list of clusters or blocks.

Inodes can be allocated or unallocated. Allocated inodes represent files which are used by the file system. The file points to the inode structure with the intent to tell the operating system where the file data can be found. The metadata on the file is filled out completely and the data of the file in the cluster or block is pointed from the inode. Unallocated inodes may or may not have the metadata filled out and the pointer to cluster or blocks of data may or may not exist. If an inode is never used by the file system, no data is ever filled out. If used but the file is deleted, the data stored on the inode is not typically wiped or overwritten.

3.5.4 File Name Layer

File names can be stored in two places: for Windows, file names can be in the file metadata (Unix does not store file names in metadata), or the directory file. File names point to the Metadata address. The File Name Layer provides a separate stricture for giving names to files. While the metadata layer describes the file, the file name layer provides a way to identify the file. The file name structure is stored as data units allocated to the parent directory. These data units contain the name of the file and the address of the metadata structure. When files are deleted, the file system will hide the name, while retaining much of the data which can be recovered.

3.6   Linux Basics

Linux is a very powerful operating system and can be complex at times. Some information pertinent to forensic investigations are:

- Account Management

- File System Management

- Executed Applications

- Network Configurations

Within the File System Layer of a Linux system, the superblock is a list of all the free space on the disk. This area of storage contains much information, particularly:

- Block size

- Total number of blocks

- Number of block per group

- Number of reserved blocks

- Total number of inodes

- Number of inodes per block group

The breakdown of the superblock is as follows (Byte Offset, Field Length, Field Name):

- 0   4 bytes   Number of Total Inodes

- 4   4 bytes   Number of Total Blocks

- 24 4 bytes   Block Size

- 32 4 bytes   Blocks in each Group

- 40 4 bytes   Inodes in each Group

- 88 2 bytes   Size of an Inode

The data layer is comprised by basic units called blocks. Multiple sectors are combined to make a block. The block size is defined during formatting of the drive and is typically 1024 bytes, 2048 bytes, or 4096 bytes. All blocks belong to a Block Group which has a redundant copy of the crucial file system superblock, group descriptor table, and part of the following:

- EXT2/3 file system block bitmap

- Inode bitmap

- Inode table

- Data blocks

Blocks are addressed, starting with Block 0. Group 0 begins immediately after the reserved blocks.

File system security in UNIX provides read, write, and execute permissions to the OWNER, GROUP, and EVERYONE.

Unix file types are:

- Regular files - contains typical software or data

- Directories - contains file names and other directories

- Named Pipes and Sockets - communicates with processes either one or two-way

- Symbolic Links - aliases to other files

- Device Files - found in the /dev directory and represent a character device (byte level access to hardware) or block device (block level access to hardware)

Each Unix file has a unique inode which contains information about the file.

Each EXT3FS file has four times associated with if and stored as the inode store time information:

- Modified - the last time the data layer was last modified.

- Accessed - the last time the data layer was accessed.

- Changed - the last time the metadata layer was modified.

- Deleted - the time the file was deleted and should match the last change time.

The modified, accessed, and changed times are commonly referred to as the MAC times.

To aid the management of data files, the inode has a listing of the blocks on the disk where the data is stored. The size of this list is fixed. The number of entries allowed is based on the file system. Entries, or pointers, come in direct and indirect types. A direct pointer simply points to where the file data is stored. A single indirect pointer will point to an area that holds 256 direct block pointer, not to the actual file data. Indirect pointers can point to areas on the disk that point to another area of the disk. These are called double and triple indirect pointers.

Directories provide a hierarchical structure. Directories are files which contain a sequence of entries as data. For every file created in a directory, the directory file contains the inode number, the file name, the size of the file name, and other variables.

In a Unix system when a file is deleted, some data may still exist on the system, such as:

- Filename Layer

    o File Name in the Directory file

    o Inode number, if not overwritten

- Metadata Layer

    o UID/GID

    o Data Modification and Access times

    o Inode Change time and Deletion time

    o Link Count

    o File type, permissions, size, and block addresses

- Data Layer

    o Data blocks will be marked unallocated but data is preserved

The Linux system will delete all links since EXT3FS was introduced.

3.6.1 Account Management

Most activities performed by investigators should be performed as a non-root user. Use the useradd command to create a new user. A "# useradd" will create a root user, while a "$ useradd" will create a non-root user. When logging in, the Linux system will enter the user's home directory. The "passwd" command is used to change passwords. Any user can change their password with "$ passwd" and root users can change the passwords of others with "# passwd". Users can switch accounts using the "su" command: if no login name is provided, the root is assumed.

3.6.2 Linux File System

The top of the file system is named "/". Several directories may be found within the file system, including:

- /bin - stores executable files

- /sbin - like /bin stores executable files

- /dev - stores device files

- /etc - stores configuration items, such as account information and hashed passwords

- /home - stores user's home directories

- /lib - stores common libraries

- /mnt - stores remote and temporary file systems

- /proc - contains the virtual file system used to store kernel information

- /tmp - stores temporary data and cleared at reboot

- /usr - stores user programs and data

- /var - stores logs

To navigate the files system, use the "cd" command. To move up the file system hierarchy, use the "cd .." command. The "pws" command will identify where in the file system the user is. To view the details on the directory or file, use the "ls" command. By default, the ls command will apply different colors to file types"

- Blue - directories

- Green - executables

- Red - compressed files

- Black - plain files

Files can be referenced using their full path or relative to where the user is currently located in the file structure. Directories can be created, using the "mkdir" command. Files can be copied using the "cp" command. To find a specific file, use the "locate" command. A search of the file system is possible using the "find" command. The "cat" command will allow the user to view the contents of a file. Files can be edited using the "mcedit" command or "gedit" command if the user has a GUI. The "less" command will allow the user to view the file by using the the arrow keys: the "q" command will exit the user out of "less".

The CD-ROM must be mounted to the system. In some Linux systems, this is done by default. When a CD-ROM is not mounted, to mount it go to the root directory and use one of the following commands:

- mount cdrom

- mount /dev/cdrom

- mount /mnt/cdrom

To eject the CD, use the "eject" command. The CD will not eject if it is currently being used.

3.6.3 Running Programs

The program's name can be entered at the command prompt to execute the program. The system will look for the program entered and the path is established through the environment variable $PATH. If the program is not in the current directory, a relative reference, "./", is required or the absolute (full) path must be identified.

The "ps" command can be used to show which processes are currently running on the machine. The columns of the output of this command include:

- User

- PID

- CPU

- Memory Utilization

- Start Time

- Time Running

- Command Line Invocation

3.6.4 Linux Networking

Network interface options can be set using the GUI tools available in the version of Linux used or by updating the file. Since several versions of the operating system are available, the best option is to update the file. The file is /etc/sysconfig/network-scripts/ifcfg-eth0. The following information should be added:

DEVICE=eth0

```
BOOTPROTO=static

BROADCAST=10.10.255.255

IPADDR=[IP address]

NETMASK=255.255.0.0

NETWORK=10.10.0.0

INBOOT-yes
```

The configuration can be viewed and changed using the "ifconfig" command. Ping and netstat commands can be used to send ICMP Echo Request messages to another host or show information about the network interfaces, respectively.

3.7   Windows File System Basics

The Windows File System has evolved and some operating systems will support multiple file systems. The first file system is FAT16 which was introduced with MS-DOS. The file allocation table (FAT) is a table maintained on the hard disk. This table provides a map of the clusters which a file is stored. The 16 at the end identifies the number of clusters that can be addressed on the file system, namely 2 to the power of 16 or 65,536 clusters. Windows 95/98/NT/2000 all support FAT16.

FAT32 was introduced with Windows 95 OSR2. Windows NT will support FAT32 with a 3rd party driver. Windows 2000/XP/2003/Vista will also support this file system. A largest hard disk available to a FAT32 file system is 2 terabytes.

Windows NT file system (NTFS) was introduced with Windows NT. Windows 2000/XP/2003/Vista will support the file system, as well as Windows 95 with a 3rd party driver.

3.7.1 FAT File Systems

FAT file systems have no security features and few time stamps. There are three variations: FAT12, FAT16, and FAT32. The primary difference between the types is the size of addressable entries. The Extended FAT file system (exFAT) was released with Windows Vista SP1 and Windows CE 6.0. FAT file systems are very reliable. A table of files and free space is kept. Because of this table, the file system will not lose data when the system crashes; though some of the data may not have been written before the crash. When this happens, CHKDSK or SCANDISK can be run to recover the lost fragments.

FAT12 file systems will support up to 4096 clusters (2 to the power of 12). Clusters can be the size of 512 bytes to 8 KB. This equates to a maximum potential file system size supported at 32 MB. A FAT32 file system will support up to 65,536 clusters. Cluster sizes range from 512 bytes to 64 KB. The maximum volume size for the file system running FAT16 is 4 GB. Both versions support the standard Windows 8.3 naming convention; that is, file names can be no more than eight characters followed by a 3 character file type reference. MS-DOS, Windows 95, Windows 98, Windows Me do not support FAT16 volumes larger than 2 GB.

FAT32 can have cluster sizes ranging from 512 bytes to 32 KB and can have up to 268,435,456 maximum addressable clusters (2 to the power of 28). This can provide a theoretical maximum volume of 8 terabytes but limited to 32 MB or 4,177,920 clusters.

FAT consists of multiple regions. An entry for each cluster is contained in the FAT area or "FAT", a table consisting of pointers to the next cluster in a file, the End of File (EOF) market or a "0" if the cluster is not being used. To read a file, the cluster is read; then the FAT table is examined for the next cluster. Cluster chains are created because every cluster has in its entry the address of the NEXT cluster. This process continues until the End of File is found.

The data area, or cluster area, is where clusters representing the data begin - specifically starting with cluster number 2. The size of the cluster is based on the size and number of sectors in the cluster. The maximum size of the data area is based on the maximum size set by the file system format. The beginning of the data area is different for FAT12/16 and FAT32 formats: Cluster 2 begins after the root directory in FAT12/16 systems, while it begins before the root directory in FAT32 systems and the root directory can exist anywhere in the data area.

The very first sector on a disk is the boot sector and performs two functions:

- Loads operating system

- Provides information about disk, such as:

- Operating system name

- Sectors per cluster

- Maximum number of root directory entries

- Volume name

- Serial number

- Size of disk

The root directory contains entries for the files and folders in the FAT file system. The number of entries in the FAT12/16 file system is preassigned and limited to 512. There is no limit in FAT32 systems.

3.7.2 NTFS File System

New Technologies File System (NTFS) provides a balance of performance, reliability, and compatibility. The 8.3 naming convention is maintained for use by DOS programs, but long file names are supported. Access to files is limited. Transaction logging is performed to provide greater ability to recover the system.

The maximum size of the volume is 16 terabytes, but can theoretically support 256 terabytes minus 64 KB The maximum size of a file can theoretically support 16 exabytes (2 to the power of 64) minus 1 KB: realistically, the supported size is 16 terabytes (2 to the power of 44) minus 64 KB. The maximum number of files supported for each volume is 4,294,967,295 files, or 2 to the power of 32 minus 1.

The NTFS boot sector is similar to the FAT boot sector, except the MFT is not in a predefined location and can be moved. If the volume will appear to be unformatted with the boot sector is corrupted and the $MFT cannot be located. The layout of the NTFS boot sector is below (Byte Offset, Field Length, Field Name):

0x00	3 bytes	Jump instruction
0x03	8 bytes	OEM ID
0x0b	25 bytes	DIOS Parameter Clock (BPB)
0x24	48 bytes	Extended BPB
0x54	426 bytes	Boot Strap Code
0x1FE	2 bytes	End of Sector Marker (0x55AA)

NTFS supports fault-tolerant disk subsystems. Three types of disk sets are supported:

- Volume set - groups free space to appear as a single volume using a single drive letter. As the volume fills up, free disk space from another partition from the same disk or another hard disk can be used to expand the volume, up to a maximum of 32 areas of free space.

- Stripe set - spans information over multiple disks in a pattern, allowing a piece of file to exist on each drive.

- Mirror set - copies every file and directory from one hard disk to another hard disk. This disk set requires two partitions, each on a different disk, and controlled by a single hard disk controller.

Clusters are the same in both FAT and NTFS systems; however in NTFS, the clusters begin at the beginning of the file system rather than the data area of the file system like the FAT system.

In NTFS, the metadata layer is enabled by the Master File Table (MFT) - a large file describing the files and directories stored in the file system. Every file and directory will have an entry in the MFT, including the MFT. Each entry in the MFT is 1024 bytes long and contains:

- MACtimes

- Security information

- File permissions

- File size

- Data clusters

Windows 95/98/ME does not track the last accessed time of the file, but 2000/NT/XP does.

Everything on a NTFS disk is a file, including the MFT. For each file, the MFT maintain a set of records called attributes. Each attribute stores a different type of data. The MFT file will track resident and non-resident attributes. Resident attributes are stored within the MFT record and stored within the file's primary MFT record. Non-resident attributes which require more space than available in the MFT record is stored outside of the MFT record. A pointer will exist in the MFT table that leads the system to the attribute.

File attributes are comprised of:

- $Standard_Information - includes timestamps, file status, and link count

- $File_Name - the file name in Unicode characters

- $Data - contains pointers to the clusters on the volume

The first 16 entries of the MFT is reserved for the NTFS volume. The entries are described below (MFT Record, File Name, Description):

0	$MFT	Master File Table
1	$MFTMIRR	Backup copy of the first four records of the MFT
2	$LOGFILE	Transactional logging file
3	$VOLUME	Serial number, creation time, and dirty flag of volume
4	$ATTRDEF	Attribute definitions
5		Root directory of the disk
6	$BITMAP	Volume's cluster map
7	$BOOT	Boot record of the volume
8	$BADCLUS	Listing of bad clusters on the volume
9	$SECURE	Security Information in Windows 2000/$Quota in NT
10	$UPCASE	Table of Unicode uppercase characters
11	$EXTEND	A directory containing $ObjId, $Quota, $Reparse, $UsnJrnl

When a file is deleted, the following information still exists on the volume:

- Filename Layer

    o   File Name in the $Filename attribute

    o   MFT number, if not overwritten

- Metadata Layer

    o   Data Modification and Access times

    o   MFT Change time and Deletion time

    o   File type, permissions, size, and cluster addresses

- Data Layer

    o   Data clusters will be marked unallocated but data is preserved

    o   Slack Space

4   Computer Investigative Laws

4.1   Legal Perspective

From an enterprise perspective the legal concerns behind the firewall relate to laws preventing hacking into systems, restricting access to stored data, and disclosure of security breaches. Laws related to data protection focus on personal data which originates inside the enterprise or on an open network, such as the Internet. When dealing with communications between the enterprise and open networks, the legal concerns are advanced to restricting the interception of communications, requirements for providing law enforcement access to communications, and retention of data on communications.

4.2   Investigators

Network security breaches are usually conducted internally by the victim, contractors typically focused on litigation, and government entities enforcing legal issues or protecting against national security threats. Any one of these groups may be investigating a single incident or all of the groups may be involved. Investigations are commonly conducted internally and the first responders play a key role in determining the situations and protecting the evidence from contamination. Often, the first responders are focused on blocking the attack and bringing the infrastructure back to a normal state; which will often prove to destroy any volatile evidence required in the investigation. Therefore, the first actions of the responders are the most critical.

An incident response policy can serve to provide the proper guidelines and expectations for first responders: particularly focused on what actions are to be taken, when those actions should be taken, and how to interact with forensic evidence and teams. The policy can provide clear direction on the powers and authority first responders have in dealing with incidents in the moment. In addition, the incident response policy can provide a list of contacts that are required to be informed of incidents and progress in restoring the infrastructure and collecting evidence, as well as, authority to make decisions beyond the powers and authority given to the first responders.

4.2.1 First Response

Generally, the greatest asset for a first response is a cool head. Panicking can cause numerous problems and mistakes to be made, such as losing evidence or informing the attacker that his actions have been discovered. Reactions to an attack must be performed quickly with the initial actions making very little changes to the system which will hinder further investigations.

A first responder's initial task is to understand the source and scope of the incident. Is the incident the result of an attack? The first responder must determine which and how many systems are affected, as well as how they are affected. Determining which system is affected is made easier when the responder can compare the original system with the current system based on forensic images created before the incident. These comparisons will allow the responder to determine what files have been added, modified, or deleted from a system. Once an affected system has been identified, the network topology and trusted relationships are clues to determining other affected systems. From log information, the responder can:

- Determine the immediate origin of the attack

- The identify of servers where data was sent, if any

- Identity of other possible victims, either upstream or downstream from the known affected system

At some point, the responder must move from discovery to actual responding to an attack. The first step is to prevent any continuing damage. Depending on the type of attack, this action may range from installing ingress filters to clock the attack, to diverting any continuing transmissions into a secure portion of the network or honeypot. In general, most actions will involve isolating critical systems or data from the attack. In many cases, these responses require consulting with management and/or legal counsel to:

- Determine the feasibility of actions

- The appropriateness of actions from a business, legal, and technical perspectives

- The best method of isolating the compromised system(s)

In incidents where the attacker is actively intruding the network, it is best to delay any actions that could tip the attacker that his presence is known. The longer the responder can track the attacker without the attacker's knowledge, the more information that can be gathered about the attacker, particularly his legitimate location. If eventually blocking the attack is the only option, the responder should ensure that no trojans or backdoors are left behind for the attacker to perform further damage. One that cannot be done because it is an illegal act is to "hack" the hacker with the intent to degrade or deny services for the attacker.

4.2.2 Internal Reporting

When an incident occurs and results of preliminary investigations finished, the appropriate people within the organization should be notified; including the security coordinator and management. Depending on the organization, policies, and the nature of the incident, legal departments and human resources may need to be notified, as well as law enforcement. Communication avenues may need to be developed and distributed to other potential victims, vendors, security vendors, and CERT.

When sending reports, protected channels of communication should be used. If the system has been compromised, these channels should not be used. The convenience of e-mail, instant messaging, chat, and other electronic communication services are often ineffective for investigations when the system has been rooted. The use of out-of-band modes to communicate is the best options. If the compromised system must be used, all communication about the incident should be encrypted. Additionally, ensure all communication, particularly telephone communications, will only reveal details related to the incident to the person(s) on the authorized list.

4.2.3 Best Practices

First responders and investigators must maintain excellent documentation from the discovery of the incident throughout the analysis of the information gathered. The notes documented will aid in future analysis and opportunities to show the evidence. Irregularities and actions to take will be easier to remember if written. The types of information which should be documented are:

- Dates and times of events related to the incident

- Description of events related to the incident

- Data and times of incident related phone calls and communications, as well as participants

- Persons working on incident-related tasks

- Description of tasks and amount of time on those tasks

- Systems, accounts, services, data, and networks affected by the incident and how they are affected

Information should be stored in a secure location to ensure that it cannot be easily alerted or destroyed. Records should be used to quantify the damage suffered because of the incident. The information related to damage should include time, money, and resources spent on:

- Investigating the nature of the incident and its source

- Identifying the vulnerabilities exploited and the appropriate fix

- Determining what data, programs, systems, or information have been accessed, altered, or destroyed

- Determining to what extent the data, programs, systems, or information have been accessed, altered, or destroyed

- Recreating modified or deleted programs, files, or data

- Reloading and reconfiguring damaged software

- Patching system to prevent future attacks of a similar nature

- Resecuring the data, programs, systems and information

4.2.4 Outsourcing Investigations

In some situations, organizations may request the assistance of outside consultants to manage investigations. When outsourcing, the investigators should be clear on the organization's policies. The same guidelines for internal investigators apply to third-party investigators. Investigators are required to be certified in some jurisdictions and must be licensed before than can engage in private investigations. The requirements for licensing vary from one jurisdiction to the next.

When using a third-party investigator, the scope of work should be clearly stated, as well as the authority the investigator has. The client should participate in the investigation and reporting to the client is paramount. Agreements for confidentiality and fidelity responsibilities should be clearly defined, as well as how issues of indemnity should be handled.

4.2.5 Law Enforcement

Investigators should consider involving law enforcement when an incident begins to look like criminal activity. Some indications that a situation involves criminal activity are:

- Unauthorized user logging into a system

- Abnormal processes running on a system using an abnormally high amount of system resources

- Virus or worm infecting the system

- Remote user attempting to penetrate the system using atypical means of access

- Heavy volume of packets bombarding the system in a short period of time

Computer crimes include:

- Using networks to commit traditional crimes

- Software privacy

- Wiretapping and snooping

- Computer fraud and abuse

4.3   Pertinent Laws

4.3.1 1996 National Information Infrastructure Protection Act

One of the most difficult problems with the rapid growth of computer technology is ensuring the laws and regulations to protect against computer crimes remain abreast of emerging technologies. This was present in 1994 when the Computer Emergency and Response Team (CERT) reported that a 498 percent increase in the number of computer intrusions and 702 percent rise in the number of sites affected by these intrusions. U.S. legislature chose to add amendments to the Computer Fraud and Abuse Act to address specific abuses from misuse of new technologies. The result is the 1996 National Information Infrastructure Protection Act.

4.3.2 President's Executive Order on Critical Infrastructure Protection

The terrorist attack on the United States on September 11, 2001 identified a number of concerns related the vulnerability of the national infrastructure. Within two months, the President of the United States issued the Executive Order on Critical Infrastructure Protection to ensure protection of information systems used for the critical infrastructure. Part of this infrastructure includes the emergency preparedness communications and the physical assets supporting the systems. In essence, the president created an official security policy for the United States.

4.3.3 USA Patriot Act of 2001

Shortly after the Executive Order mentioned above, Congress passed Public Law 107-56, titled the "Uniting and Strengthening America by Providing Appropriate Tools Required to Intercept and Obstruct Terrorist Act or 2001." It's short name is the USA Patriot Act. The law covers several items pertinent to IT solutions or the use of IT in dealing with terrorist activity, including:

- Title II authorizes the interception of wire, oral, and electronic communication to produce evidence of terrorism offenses, computer fraud and abuse.

- Title III focuses on monetary transactions used in supporting terrorist activities.

- Title IV provides guidelines of border control and immigration laws involving electronic sharing of intelligence.

- Title V provides guidelines for removing obstacles when investigating terrorism.

- Title VII covers increasing information sharing for critical infrastructure protection.

- Title VIII strengthens criminal laws as they apply to terrorism.

4.3.4 Homeland Security Act of 2002

Another result of 9/11 was the creation of the Department of Homeland Security, a government agency charged with the following tasks:

- Control U.S. borders and prevent terrorists from entering.

- Quick and effective response to emergencies in cooperation with state and local authorities.

- Develop technologies to detect and protect from biological, chemical, and nuclear weapons.

- To provide a single daily report of threats from intelligence and information from several law enforcement agencies.

The act creating this government agency was the Homeland Security Act of 2002.

4.3.5 Computer Fraud and Abuse Act

U.S. legislation, 18 U.S.C. § 1030 (Computer Fraud and Abuse Act), defines the activities that are considered felony offenses of computer fraud and abuse. It also describes the actions available to law enforcement in investigating and apprehending suspects of computer fraud and abuse. Passed in 1986 and updated in 1996, the act prohibits the intentional and unauthorized access of any protected computer if the attacker obtains government or financial information. A protected computer is considered any computer which is used by the federal government, a financial institution, or affects the interstate or foreign communication or commerce of the United States.

The act defines damage as any impairment to the integrity or availability of data, programs, system or information. A violation of the act requires proof that the attacker or his behavior has caused:

- Loss of $5000 to one or more persons over a one year period.

- Modification or impairment of medical examinations, diagnosis, treatment, or care of one of more individuals or records.

- Physical injury to any person.

- Threat to public health or safety.

- Damage affecting a computer system used by or for the government.

Any reasonable cost to the victim can be attributed to the financial limits set by the act, including the cost to:

- Respond to the offense

- Conduct a damage assessment

- Restore data, programs, system, or other information prior to attack

- Lost revenue

- Consequential damage from service interruption

Losses can be aggregated across multiple computers and victims to reach the cost threshold if the losses are accrued because of related course of conduct.

Additionally, intent of the attacker must be demonstrated. Intent is describes as knowingly transmitting a program, information, code, or command which intentionally causes damage to a protected computer. This applies to anyone, including employees or hackers. The maximum penalty for first-time offenders is a fine and 10 years imprisonment. However, reckless conduct only applies to persons outside the network who do not have authorization

47

to access resources. The maximum penalty for reckless conduct for first-time offenders is a fine and 5 years imprisonment. If the act was neither intentional nor reckless, the maximum penalty for first-time offenders is a fine and 1 year imprisonment. This applies to outside offenders only.

4.3.6 Electronic Communications Privacy Act (ECPA)

The Electronic Communications Privacy Act (ECPA) governs the accessibility of stored electronic communication for law enforcement. Three main categories of stored electronic communication:

- Stored content of communications

- Stored communications associated data

- Subscriber and billing information, and certain session-specific information

The ECPA (18 U.S.C. §§ 2701-12) provides governance on accessing and disclosing stored files. The act will impose restrictions on and grant rights to system operators, government agents, and anyone responsible for accessing and disclosing stored customer information.

Information about stored information on communications is protected by the ECPA. Specifically, restrictions are placed on providers for when information can be voluntarily disclosed to law enforcement. Differences exist of public providers and private providers. Public providers are those entities which provide general services to the public and not a specific group within the populace; while private providers offer services only to a select qualifying individual, such as employer/employee or school/faculty and/or students.

Public providers cannot generally voluntarily offer information to law enforcement without violating the act. This means, that law enforcement must utilize the legal process to obtain information on an incident. Before disclosing any information to the government, a public provider must review any statutory exceptions which allow the provider to volunteer communication content if:

- Consent to provide exists

- The rights and property of the customers are protected

- The contents are inadvertently obtained and pertained to the commission of a crime

- The danger of death or serious physical information is reasonably perceived by the provider in an emergency situation

The same basic restrictions apply to information about the subscriber without disclosing the content of any communications, such as network activity. One exception is that the information can be disclosed to any person other than a governmental entity.

Private providers do not have this restriction: they can offer information to law enforcement without any violation to the act occurring. However, they may be restricted from disclosing information because of some contractual obligation or other government regulations. If a private provider does not voluntarily disclose any information, law enforcement must use the legal process to obtain any data.

4.3.7 United States Wiretap Act

The U.S. Wiretap Act (18 U.S.C. § 2511) prohibits the intentional interception, use, or disclosure of wire and electronic communications without a statutory exception. This act protects the contents of electronic and voice communication. There are a number of exceptions that are defined by the act as acceptable situations for wiretaps: the three primary reasons are:

- Provider Exception - allows providers to conduct broad monitoring of electronic communications which is reasonable to ensure their rights or property are protected or as the result of the normal course of employment by the tapping individual. This is a limited exception and cannot be misused for criminal investigations.

- Consent of a Party - authorizes the interception of communications if one of the parties consents to the interception (some U.S. states require the consent of all parties). Consent can be in the form of a written consent of authorized users or as a network banner clearly displayed before a user uses resources on the network.

- Computer Trespasser Exception - allows law enforcement to intercept communications to and from "computer trespassers" even when the system the trespasser is using is a pass-through system. A computer trespasser is any person using a protected computer without authorization and cannot be a person known by the provider as having an existing contract with the provider for use for the system. In addition to the restriction for acquiring communications to and from the computer trespasser applying, the act specifies that the consent of the systems owner must be obtained; the interception must be pursuant to an investigation and must be conducted by the government or one of its agents.

4.3.8 Pen/Trap Statute

The Pen Registers and Trap and Trace Device statute (18 U.S.C. §§ 3121-3127) governs collection on non-content traffic information associated with communications in real-time. According to the statute, a pen register is any device or process that records or decodes dialing, routing, addressing, or signaling information transmitted by an instrument or facility where wire or electronic communications are made, unless related to billing or accounting purposes. A trap and trace device is any device or process capturing information electronic or other impulses which identify the originating number or other dialing, routing, addressing, and signaling information used to identify the source of the communication.

The statute applies to header information of a communication and not the content of the communication. The statute does not apply to providers who use pen/trap devices related to the operation, maintenance, and testing of wire or electronic communication service or protection of the provider's rights and property, or to the users of the provider's services. The statute allows providers to record the initiation or completion of a wire or electronic communication for the purpose of protecting the provider, other providers furnishing services to complete the communication or the user of the service from fraudulent, unlawful or abusive use of the service. Consent of the user for the service can be obtained to allow the provider from being liable when using pen/trap devices.

4.3.9 COE Treaty

In June of 2001, the Council on Europe draft Convention on Cybercrime approved a treaty for ratification by the individual European states. The ratification process is still in process. Some of the topics covered by the treaty are:

- Offenses against the confidentiality, integrity, and availability of computer data and systems

- Computer-related offences

- Content-related offences

- Offenses related to infringements of copyright and related rights

- Ancillary liability and sanctions

4.3.10   Legislation for Lawful Access

In addition to the Wiretap Act and the Pen/Trap Act, other laws have been enacted to deal with the complex challenges of technologies in communications. The United States has enacted the Communications Assistance to Law Enforcement Act which provides guidance to the Federal Communication Commission (FCC) on the capabilities and capacities required by service providers to monitoring their networks. The United Kingdom has similar guidelines with their Regulation of Investigatory Powers Act (RIPA).

These statutes generally require services provides to have permanent capabilities to monitor certain traffic types on the network. They provide guidelines for creating the ability to isolate specific target subscribers.

In the European Union, the Data Retention Directive (2006/24/EC) requires service providers to store communication data, not content of communication, of EU customers. The retention periods can be set by member states and range from 6 months to 24 months. The directive applies to all ISPs, fixed-line, and mobile service providers.

4.3.11   Health Insurance Portability and Accountability Act (HIPAA)

The Health Insurance Portability and Accountability Act (HIPAA) protect the privacy of patient health information maintained by "covered entities". The act does this by creating national privacy rules for handling Protected Health Information (PHI) while protecting the confidentiality, integrity, and availability of the information there a Security Rule.

Covered entities are health plans, health care clearinghouses, and certain health care providers. If a covered entity fails to comply with the rules of the act, they are subject to penalties up to $250,000 and/or a jail term of up to 10 years. Violations can be the result of a single employee's actions, and therefore it is important for persons responsible for acquiring, maintaining, or distributing information to consult with legal departments to verify the process is compliant with the HIPAA Security Rule.

4.3.12   Computer Misuse Act 1990

The primary anti-hacking law in the United Kingdom is the Computer Misuse Act 1990. The act defines three offenses:

- Section 1 - Unauthorized access to computer materials: pertains to situations where a person knowingly uses one computer to unauthorized access data on another computer.

- Section 2 - Unauthorized access with the intent to commit or facilitate commission of further offenses.

- Section 3A - Unauthorized acts with intention to impair operations of computer.

- Section 3B - Making, supplying or obtaining articles for use in offenses under section 1 or 3.

4.3.13   German Criminal Code

The primary legislation against network crimes in Germany is the German Criminal Code (Strafgesetzbuch). The following offenses are defined:

- Section 201 (eavesdropping) - covers the eavesdropping and recording of the spoken word of another person in a location other than public and using the recorded information, publishing it, or providing it to a third party.

- Section 202a (spying out data) - covers unauthorized access to data not intended for the attacker, which is stored or will be transmitted using encryption or other method of protection.

- Section 206 (violation of post or telecommunications secrecy) - covers any interference with or disclosure of information subject to post or telecommunications secrecy, including blocking of emails.

- Section 263a (computer fraud) - covers any fraud committed through the result of data processing being influenced by the incorrect design of a computer program, incorrect or incomplete data use, unauthorized use of data, or unauthorized interference.

- Section 269 (Forgery of data relevant for proof) - covers the storage or modification of data related to legal proof for the purpose of forging legal relations.

- Section 303a (modification of data) - covers the deletion, suppression or modification of data, or making data unusable whether stored or being transmitted with protection.

- Section 303b (computer sabotage) - covers the interruption of data processing essential for a company or public authority.

- Section 317 (interruption of operation of telecommunications equipment) - covers the interruption of operations of telecommunications equipment which serves the public through destroying, damaging, removing, or modifying computers or disconnection of electric power.

4.4   EU Legal Position

4.4.1 European Union

The European Union is comprised of 27 Member States, which are:

- Austria
- Belgium
- Bulgaria
- Cyprus
- Czech Republic
- Denmark
- Estonia
- Finland
- Germany
- Greece
- Hungary
- Ireland
- Italy
- Latvia
- Lithuania
- Luxembourg
- Malta
- Netherlands
- Poland
- Portugal
- Romania

- Slovakia

- Slovenia

- Spain

- Sweden

- United Kingdom

Other countries follow EU and various respects and make up the European Economic Area (EEA). The countries include:

- Iceland

- Liechtenstein

- Norway

The European Union is comprised of three pillars and therefore not a single legal entity (though the proposed European Constitution will change this). The pillars are the European Communities, Common Foreign and Security Policy, and Justice and Home Affairs. EU institutions are found within these pillars and have various roles and powers among the member states. The key institutions are:

- Council of Ministers - represents the Member States

- European Parliament - represents the people

- European Commission - the central authority

- European Court of Justice - the central court

Computer crimes are under the authority of the law enforcement focus in Member States, the EU Council of Ministers (third pillar), and the economic focus of the European Economic Community (first pillar). Member States generally have legislative authority for most issues related to computer crimes. The legal systems of the Member States fall into two categories:

- Common Law (England) - both legislation and court decisions provide binding legal force

- Civil Law (Germany) - only legislation has binding legal force

4.4.2 Data Protection

Data protection is the largest source of litigation issues. Most data protection laws will in some way restrict the processing of personal data. Processing is defined as any activity on data in electronic or physical form. Personal data refers to any information identifying an individual.

The responsibility for enforcing data protection law is often laid on any entity which acquires and processes personal data (data controllers) or entities that process data on behalf of data controllers (data processers).

The European Union has issued two directives regarding data protection. The first directive is called the "Data Protection Directive" (95/46/EC) and covers the processing of all types of personal data. The second directive is the "Privacy and Electronic Communications Directive or PEC Directive (2002/58/EC) and applies specific rules for processing personal data associated with electronic communications. Each Member State of the European Union implements the directives and each Member State has a national data protection authority (DPA) who is responsible for enforcing the data protection law within the state. The interpretations and aggressiveness of the directive implementation can varies from one Member State to the next.

The key principles of data protection law are:

- Notice and Consent - data processors are accountable to data subjects to communicate what personal data is being processed and how that data is processed.

- Security of Processing - personal data must be secure at all times.

- Access - Data subjects have the right to access individually the personal data about them and correct any mistakes found.

- Foreign Transfer - when personal data is transferred outside the EEA, it is subject to additional restrictions and requirements.

With the data protection law, all Member States are required to adopt sanctions for any improper access to personal data. According to Article 17 of the Data Protection Directive, "the controller must implement appropriate technical and organizational measures to protect personal data against accidental or unlawful destruction or accidental loss, alteration, unauthorized disclosure or access." If this is not followed, three different types of liability may be triggered:

- Article 22 - covers a person's right to judicial remedy for any breach of rights guaranteed by national law.

- Article 23 - covers the compensation by the Member State to any person who has suffered damage by unlawful processing operations or any act incompatible with the national provisions adopted to comply with the Directive.

- Article 24 - covers the need for sanctions for any case of infringement of the provisions adopted to comply with the Directive.

4.4.3 Criminal Conduct

The Information Systems Attacks Decision (2005/222/JHA) provides greater cohesion to Member State laws related to attacks on information systems and criminalizes the following offenses:

- Article 2 - Illegal access to information systems: covers any intentional access without right or authority to an information system.

- Article 3 - Illegal system interference: covers the intentional hindrance or interruption of information system functions by inputting, transmitting, damaging, deleting, deteriorating, altering, suppressing or rendering inaccessible any computer data.

- Article 4 - Illegal data interference: covers the intentional deletion, damaging, deterioration, alteration, suppression, ore rendering inaccessible any computer data.

- Article 5 - Instigation, aiding and abetting, and attempt: must be found guilty of the above offences.

4.5   Acquiring Data

The goal of data acquisition during an investigation is to secure all relevant data without changing the relevant aspects of the data or compromising the investigation. Relevant data will either suggest guilt (inculpatory) or suggest innocence (exculpatory). If data is missing, it should be noted.

Acquiring data must be performed by individuals who have the authority to conduct the investigation. Without the proper permissions, the results of any investigative work may not be used or admissible; activities performed without permission may lead to loss of employment and even lawsuit for violating rights of privacy.

4.5.1 Granting Authority

Permissions should be well documented for internal investigators, outside contractors, and law enforcement. The incident response policy and job descriptions are the basis for defining permissions for internal investigators. The incident response policy should be reflected in contracts with outside contractors. The guidelines for law enforcement are typically set by government agencies and must follow the legal process.

Authority should be defined for acquiring stored data on stand-alone machines or the network, or in real-time across the network. Authority can also be assigned across all situations.

Before seizing, duplicating, or analyzing a stand-alone storage device the source of authority should be understood. Typical source of authority includes:

- Consent of the owner of abandonment by the owner

- Outsourcing contract

- Terms of service with subscriber

- Legal process, including search warrant

When conducting investigations, the more information that can be acquired, the better the analysis and conclusions from that analysis. The best option is creating a image of the device to capture the hidden files and directories, swap data, deleted data, and slack space. Additionally, hash values for the original and image can be useful. With an image, thorough analysis can be conducted and the strength of the conclusions can be tested. Backup media can provide useful information about the original system and data. Unfortunately, such extensive data acquisition is practical or even necessary.

Logging is a form of data acquisition commonly seen in networks. There are two types of logging:

- Accessing stored content of a communication or stored information about a communication

- Real-time monitoring (eavesdropping) f the content of a communication

Acquiring stored data from the network is usually more complicated than acquiring stored data from stand-alone machines. Regulations provide restrictions on data acquisitions over the network for different types of data, namely the Electronic Communications Privacy Act (ECPA), the Health Insurance Portability and Accountability Act (HIPAA), and Sarbanes-Oxley (SOX).

4.6   Data Preservation

4.6.1 Chain of Custody

How data is acquired is important in maintaining the integrity of the information and the acceptance of evidence in legal matters. However, it is only the beginning: the next step is preserving the data. Data needs to be stored and protected from alteration. The process of preserving the integrity of data is called the chain of custody.

The chain of custody ensures that the person handling the evidence is always known: if the data changes hands, the transfer is documented. In addition to the transfer, the chain of custody also documents what changes are made to the evidence, including no changes have been made. Since copies of the original evidence should be used for analysis, any copies made should be recorded and the original left unchanged.

The burden of the chain of custody is on the party responsibile for offering the evidence into trial. Legally, access to a copy of an evidence item, rather than the item itself, may not be accounted for in the chain of custody when admitted at trial. If a break in the chain occurs, a missing link, the evidence could be inadmissible but not necessarily. Most courts will allow the evidence with a missing link if sufficient proof is in place that the evidence is what it claims to be. Additionally, not everyone in the chain of custody will automatically be required to testify in court. A form can be used and consulted by a witness to establish the chain of custody. The chain of custody can be established by the witness by testifying on habit or routine. The form can be basic with the following information:

- Item name

- Item description

- Date

- Action taken

- Received by

- Notes

Part of establishing a reliable chain of custody is maintaining the evidence in a secure location. Electronic data may be stored on a server. Whatever the location, only persons authorized to have access should be granted access. A documented procedure should be known to all authorized persons on how evidence is stored and retrieved from the secure location. Records showing that the process is followed will protect against any charges that the evidence is untrustworthy because it was altered.

4.7   Investigative Reports

Investigators may be required to prepare a report. The format of the report is at the discretion of the organization. Depending on the audience of the report, the format may differ though the differences should contain the same basic information. Forensics reports can eventually become key to a court case, whether for the prosecution or the defense.

The key to writing investigative reports is to be clear and accurate. Because of how they are used, the reports should be professional, not slang. Opinions must be supported by the evidence. Prejudice or bias perspectives should not be found in the report.

When drafting the reports, investigators should consider the audience. A lot of technical jargon will distract average people from understanding the contents of the report. However, not enough technical jargon could underestimate the viability of the investigation. Pictures, such as screen shots, can provide sufficient explanation for hard concepts. Investigators should always be mindful of the possibility the report will be used in court and ensure that the contents of the report will not create any legal questions. Conclusions in the report should reflect the scientific methods used in the analysis.

The best reports have the following attributes:

- Conclusions are derived from using sound methods.

- The results reflected are repeatable and reliable.

- The method of analysis is thorough and unbiased.

- Work is documented such that it can be replicated.

The primary audience of a report will either be corporate and/or law enforcement entities. Corporate entities can include management, systems administrators, and peers. Prosecutors, judges, jurors, and witnesses are all members of law enforcement. It is important to understand what the audience wants or expects to be covered in the report.

The process of analysis should be well documented. The steps of work must be clear and repeatable. Nothing should be stated which cannot be proved.

4.8   Presentation

Legal evidence has some basic rules:

- Relevance - all admissible evidence must be relevant to a specific issue in the trial and it is the burden of the submitting party to prove its relevance.

- Authentication - all admissible evidence must be what it claims to be, which can be proven by the chain of custody.

- Unaltered - all admissible evidence should demonstrate evidence that no tampering or alterations have been made: some techniques are hash values, write blockers, chain of custody forms, and testimony.

- Best Evidence - Evidence must be original: presented evidence must accurately reflect the data.

4.8.1 Testimony

When witnesses are required in a court case, there are two types which may be experienced:

- Lay witness - has personal knowledge of the issue and can testify to the source of the facts in the case. No special skill is required and opinions are allowed only when they are based on the witness's perception, helpful to clearly understand the testimony, and not based on scientific, technical, or other specialized knowledge which could make the witness an expert witness.

- Expert witness - requires special skill and little to no personal knowledge of the issue. Opinions are allowed as long the following requirements are satisfied: testimony is based on sufficient data or facts, the testimony is the result of reliable methods and principles, which are applied reliably to the facts of the case.

In the United States, two tests are applied to expert opinions to allow them to be admissible in court: Dauber and Frye. The Dauber test focuses on the reliability and relevance of expert evidence, requiring at least four factors to be in place to demonstrate reliability:

- Techniques used have been and can be tested.

- Techniques have been reviewed by peers and been published.

- The error rates for the techniques are known.

- Techniques are generally accepted in the relevant community.

The Frye test is concerned with the acceptance of scientific techniques in the community.

4.9   Honeypots

Honeypots are essentially fake networks: that is, non-production servers which look like production servers with the intent to attract attackers and hackers. The actions of any intruders are monitored by various devices, including firewalls, sniffers, IDS systems. The data is analyzed. Honeypots are placed in networks under a number of configurations: they can be independent of the production networks and used to monitor malicious activity which is aimed at it or directed towards it or the honeypot can hide within the production servers.

4.9.1 Legal Considerations

The use of honeypots has not been tested legally, and some consequences may arise when using them. Some legal concerns involve the monitoring of traffic being similar to any illegal interception of communication in violation of the Wiretap act.

Additionally by having the honeypot in place to attract attackers, if the honeypot is used by the attacker to attack system downstream, the operator of the honeypot may be found liable to the downstream victims for facilitating the attack and failing to protect the system from attack. An operator may be found liable when attacks on others is known but those victims are not notified. And if the honeypot is used to store or distribute contraband, such as pornography, liability may fall with the operator.

Finally, entrapment is another legal concern related to the use of honeypots. Though the legal definition of entrapment would only pertain to honeypots established by law enforcement, the concept of entrapment raises considerations about the "system protection" exception to the Wiretap Act.

4.9.2 Wiretap Act and Honeypots

The Wiretap Act provides broad protection against the intentional interception, use, or disclosure of wire and electronic communications unless a statutory exception can be applied. Honeypots can be configured to monitor all packets sent from or to the system. For the monitoring of all packet information and content to be legal under the Wiretap Act, at least one of the exceptions must apply: for monitoring of only non-content information, the rules of the Pen/Trap stature must apply.

Though the Wiretap Act contains many exceptions, they may or may apply to an even greater number of situations. Until an exception can be applied, the act prohibits the real-time monitoring of content which is the function of a honeypot. Several exceptions should be considered when using honeypots:

- Computer Trespasser

- Party to the Communication

- Consent of a Party

- Provider Protection

The computer trespasser exception applies to government applications and states that a trespasser can be monitored if:

- No contractual relationship or authority exists on the computers

- The provider authorizes interception

- The monitoring is performed by the government

- Only the trespasser's communications are intercepted

- Interception is relevant to an ongoing investigation

Honeypots typically have no authorized users; therefore all who access the honeypots are trespassers. Since the provider is deploying the honeypot, they are authorizing any interceptions through the honeypot. Monitoring must be performed by a law enforcement entity or person acting "under color of law." Additionally, all communications through the honeypots would consist of transmission by trespassers or those consenting to the monitoring. As for the ongoing investigation clause, it is the essence of honeypots to provide ongoing monitoring for potential attackers. If all of these can be proven by the provider, honeypots could fall into the computer trespasser exception and remain legal.

With the consent of party exception, the Wiretap Act allows monitoring where the interception is performed by a party of the communication or the party gives prior consent to the interception. Two methods are available to investigators for obtaining consent. The first method is to have a logon banner deployed, as with all production servers, where the user attempting to access the honeypot must consent to monitoring. An attacker who sees the banner and continues to use the server will be consenting to the monitoring. Unfortunately, it is not possible to deploy a banner to all ports on a system: therefore, an attacker may be able to access the system through a unbannered port and never see the banner. The operator may close those unbannered ports and ensure no traffic passes through them; however, one goal of a honeypot is to investigate attacks through unbannered ports. Additionally, the deployment of a banner may conflict with the intended "attractiveness" of the server.

The second method of obtaining consent understands that when a honeypot is under attack, the system is party to the communication with the attacker. As a result, the honeypot operator may provide consent on behalf of the honeypot for the interception. However, when the attacker is using the honeypot as a pass-through system to other systems, the party of the communication concept becomes hazy and can cause some risk of litigation. Some operators have placed rate-limiting mechanisms to limit the amount of outbound traffic from the honeypot, and therefore reducing the chance of the honeypot being used a platform for further attacks downstream.

The provider exception allows a provider the right to intercept and monitor communications with the intent to prevent misuse of the system resulting in damage, theft, or invasions of privacy. Under this exception, interceptions seem legal; but the use of honeypots under this exception has been untested. The problem arises in the subjective and objective factors are deploying a honeypot for the purpose of protecting the rights and property of the operator. Is the honeypot really self-defense or is the operator "picking a fight" by attracting attackers? Is the honeypot related to production systems or non-production systems such as research and development? Have the attackers struck before? As a result, the provider exception may have some limited application to the use of honeypots.

4.9.3 ECPA and Honeypots

The Electronic Communications Privacy Act may provide some acceptance of honeypots, as well as some limitations. The ECPA restricts the voluntary disclosing the contents of communications and files stored a system. This restriction applies to Electronic Communications Services (ECS) and Remote Computing Services (RCS).

ECS allow authorized users the ability to send and receive wire or electronic communications. A honeypot that allows this operates as an ECS. The prohibitions apply only to operators providing services to the public. Therefore, a honeypot operating as an ECS can disclose the communications to others as long as the services are not offered to the public.

An RCS is computer storage or processing services to the public. A honeypot offering this service "to the public" is considered an RCS. If the services are not provided to the public, the EPCA restrictions do not apply as an RCS.

5 Forensic Methodology

5.1 Incident Response

Forensic incident response has a primary goal of gathering as much volatile evidence as possible before it is lost or corrupted. Most tools and techniques can be used on a variety of operating systems; but no single forensic solution is universal enough to examine every type of incident. Two categories of forensic toolkits exist:

- Evidence acquisition - saves data from a system to enable lab-based analysis

- Evidence analysis - used to find evidence on a live system or on data generated by the data acquisition tools

5.1.1 Required Equipment

When responding to an incident initially, the investigator should bring a small package of equipment. Within this package, the following items should be included:

- Small hub/switch

- CAT5 cable

- Cross-over cable

- Incident response floppy or CD-ROM

- Drive Adapters for SATA/IDE/SCSI

- Large Capacity USB/Firewire Portable Drive

Having this equipment available when responding will ensure that analysis of the live system is possible. The incident response floppy disk or CD-ROM is used to search and gather evidence security without affecting the system. Most programs are built dynamically using shared libraries. The disk will typically include execute tools from Helix3 Pro and part of SIFTKIT. The following tools, as a minimum, should be on the disk for the different operating systems:

Unix	Windows
Netstat, dd, find, ls, ps, lsof, strings, last, ifconfig, uptime	NT Resource Kit, cmd.exe

5.1.2 Forensic Tools

Several tools are used to gather evidence on a system. The three possible functions of the tools are:

- Incident Response and Verification

- Preservation of Integrity

- Evidence Collection

The landscape of tools for each of these functions under each operating system:

Incident response	Helix3 Pro, lsof, nc	Helix, WFT
Preservation of integrity	md5sum	Md5sum.exe
Evidence collection	Memdump, dd, dc3dd	Win32dd, dd.exe

Helix3 Pro is a multi-platform evidence acquisition tool. It can work with Mac OS X, Windows, and Linux environments with a single interface to allow:

- The creation of forensic images of all internal devices

- The creation of forensic images of physical memory

- Determine disk level encryption is enabled

The tool allows response on live systems, as well as acquisition and analysis of evidence on live and dead systems. The package can be obtained from www.e-fense.com. It includes several open source forensic applications, including:

- SleuthKit

- LinEn

- Libewf + mount_ewf

- Carvfs

- cryptsetup

- Truecrypt

- lvm2

- Scalpel

65

- Foremost

- LibPff

- Volatility (plus plugins)

- moto4lin

- gmobilemedia

- gammu

- gnokii

- frag_find

- pythonraw

- ptfinder

The use of a Helix3 Pro CD is similar to a standard CD distribution. It will boot into either graphics or text mode.

Netcat can be used to collect data across a network to avoid writing to the victim system's media. This can be done be using a cross-over cable from the system to the forensic workstation. A server/client architecture is used with the netcat listener on the forensic workstation and the necessary tools executed on the victim machine and piping to the listener.

5.1.3 Memory Searches

When starting the investigation, some basic knowledge is required about the file system, volatile data, hidden directories, and a timeline with the last file modifications and access times. The volatile data gathered should be what is in system memory and information about network connections and process information. System memory contains information on all the processes, files, and directories siting in residual memory. This information can be used to reconstruct the old history and identify the commands a previous individual may have executed on the system. Email and web activities can be discovered, as well as data on existed processes. Passwords collected in clear text may be found in the memory. Further investigation includes performing string searches using the dirty word list.

Win32dd.exe can be used to create a forensic image of the physical memory. The image will be in raw format. To ensure the integrity of the image, an MD5 hash is automatically created with the output.

Memparser is used in Window 2000 environments to examine a memory image and find pointers to processes with the intent to create a process list. The list can be used to examine the environment and memory of a specific process. Other operating systems require other tools: VolaTools (XP SP2/SP3 only) and Windows Memory Forensics Toolkit. Volatility is a tool framework that can be used to analyze volatile memory images using digital methods. Memoryze uses batch scripts to analyze a memory image or live machine.

5.1.4 Evidence Integrity

It is essential for forensic investigations to ensure evidence collected is not changed during the forensic process. Every copy of the digital evidence should have some method to verify that no unauthorized changes are made. Cryptic hashes can be attached to the images to ensure integrity. Hashes are cryptographic algorithms and are non-reversible. It is mathematically improbable to find the same hash function being used for two different files.

The command, md5sum, provides a 16 byte signature to the content of a binary file. When hashing data, the investigator is collecting the signature of the data to verify that no changes have been made to the data. Using the command, individual partitions and evidence disks can be hashed.

Hashing is not required for admissibility of evidence into court. However, it provides some benefits:

- Expert witnessing - as a deposed expert witness, performing best practices is essential for ensuring the acceptance of evidence: hashing is considered a best practice.

- Tampering - hashing provides substantial proof that the evidence submitted in a court case has not been tampered with or change.

- Law vs. Science - science is consistent, while law is based on human interpretation and perspective. Using the same evidence, the same analysis, and the same conclusions, most courts will rule the same way; but there is always at least one court which will rule differently.

5.2   Evidence Acquisition

The image creation process includes:

- Creating a true bit image and reading images as "read-only."

- Documenting the activities of gathering the evidence and providing a hash.

- Providing a chain of custody for gathered evidence.

There is no standard imaging methodology, because there is not a standard hardware platform nor a standard software tool set. The hardware and software available to the investigator will impact the methodology. Additionally, different rules are applied when attempting to image a live system or dead system. When responding to incidents, in most cases, the investigator will come to powered on, or live, systems. With live systems, more unknown conditions exist. On the other hand, law enforcement typically will arrive to a dead system or will obtain evidence from an incident response team.

Each piece of evidence should be labeled and data as soon as it is obtained. The tag should include the casename and evidence number or the date and evidence number. The recommended tag is the data and evidence number in the format - YYYYMMDD-##. Because a system must go back into production, a copy of the evidence is all that will be available to the investigation. The first copy of the evidence is always considered the "best evidence." The best evidence should be secured and never touched or analyzed. It will be used to make all other copies of the evidence when the original evidence is damaged. The second copy of the evidence is considered the "working copy" and used to perform analysis.

In most cases, imaging the entire physical drive is the best option for creating the best evidence. However in some cases, particularly Windows, logical drives may need to be imaged. With physical drive imaging, the entire drive is imaged. This image is always considered the best evidence. When imaging a RAID system with multiple hard drives, logical backups are appropriate. A similar RAID system is required and each logical drive is imaged onto separate media.

In Linux, drives are easily recognized, as they are all referenced as /dev/hda or /dev/sda. In Windows, the first physical drive is referred to as \\.\PhysicalDrive0 and subsequent drives identified as 1, 2, 3 and so on. With logical volumes, the partition is known as /dev/hda1 or /dev/sda1. In Windows, the logical drive is known by a drive letter (the primary drive being C:). The entire drive is known as \\.\C:.

All the data gathered must be stored. There are several formats that can be used to store data. Some allow the metadata to be stored. Some allow data to be compressed. Formats can be open or proprietary. Open formats allow different tools to use disk images, proprietary formats will limit what can be done to the data. Some common image formats include:

- Raw - the most common format is simply a copy of the hard disk data with no metadata or compression. This is also called the "dd" format.

- E01 - created by Guidance Software, (EnCASE) and is a proprietary format which will store metadata and compress data.

- AFF (Advanced Forensic Format - an open format which stores metadata and compressed data. There are three variations which allow data to be stored in a single large file (AFF), multiple small files (AFD), or as a drive image in raw format and a second file with metadata (AFM).

Write blockers are used to prevent accidental writes to source data. Though its use is good in the long term, software must be installed or the system powered off and hard drive removed. In either case, evidence may be lost.

5.2.1 Acquisition Methods

Three methods are typically seen for acquiring evidence:

- Hardware

- Helix3 Pro

- Live

In some cases, the investigator will be given a hard drive and some background information. The first thing to do is image the hard drive. To gather evidence, the required adapter will need to be attached to the hard drive, than plugged into the forensic workstation. The hard drive will need to be imaged to an image file. The image file can reside on the forensic workstation or another attached large capacity hard drive.

If the hard drive is not removed from the victim system, the system can be booted from the Helix3 Pro CDROM. This activity will not modify the hard drives of the system. Any volatile evidence should be obtained between powering the system off or rebooting the system. An image file can be stored on a large capacity USB/Firewire drive attached to the system or across the network using netcat or utilizing existing file shares.

A live evidence acquisition scenario will take a snapshot of the current hard drive. A large capacity USB/Firewire drive will need to be attached to the system or an image needs to be created over the network. The greatest advantage is the retrieval of volatile information.

The utility, dd, can be used to read input files from block to block. It is typically the first tool used to collect evidence. With this utility, any data marked deleted can be captured in the file system metadata retrieved. Three versions are commonly used:

- dd

- dd.exe

- dc3dd

Originally designed for Linux systems, dd.exe is for Windows use. The utility can copy a single file, part of a file, an entire logical disk, or physical disk. It can be used as a backup system and allows copying of the physical drive from ram, image swap files or pagefiles. If using dd.exe in Windows, the netcat utility does not need to be used.

A few basic arguments exist for dd.exe. Below is the syntax for the command:

dd.exe if=*IFILE* of=*OFILE* bs=*blocksize* count=X conv=noerror,sync

where

if = input file

of = output file

bs = block size

count = copies only X input blocks

conv=noerror,sync = skips unreadable sections

Some useful options to be used with dd.exe are:

--cryptsum *<hashtype>*	Provides hash in form of md5, sha, or sha256
--verify	Verifies the hash
--cryptout *<file>*	Writes to output file
--log *<file>*	Writes to output log file
--localwrt	Allows writing to local drive
--ata_hpa	Temporarily disables host protection

The dc3dd utility is an improved utility with additional options over dd for Linux or dd.exe for Windows, including:

progress=on	Displays a progress meter
hash=<type>	Adds the sha512 to hash capabilities
hashlog=filename	Performs integrity checks when imaging and writing to logfile
hashwindow=NUM	Performs an MD5 hash on every num bytes of data

Dd and dc3dd can be used to wipe a hard drive: to erase all data from the drive. Only one pass on the drive is required: the source if= should be set to /dev/zero, causing the device to write a 00 byte to every byte on the drive.

ATA, or IDE, disks have a reserved area at the end of the drive that cannot be read or written to by a user. Commonly known as the Host Protected Area, its purpose was to allow computer companies to store restoration files and data that could not be deleted by a user. Anyone can create this area and it cannot be copied by acquisition tools. If an HPA exists on the disk, the resulting image file from dd will be smaller than the reported size of the disk.

To detect the HPA, low-level ATA commands are required: namely comparing two reports for the actual size of the disk and the size available for use by the user or operating system. Known as the maximum disk sector and the maximum user sector respectively, the different in the sizes will be the HPA. The disk_stat tool can detect the disk sizes in Linux only. To check the disk size of a Windows machine using Linux tools, it is required to boot into Helix 3 Pro or to attach a detached hard drive to the analysis workstation. Dd.exe has a detection and removal option, as well.

To remove the HPA, the maximum user sector can be set to the same size as the maximum disk sector. This can be done using the disk_sreset command for Linux systems only. Two versions are available: one to make the change temporarily and another to make it permanently. The Linux command mentioned is the temporary version and the HPA will be reset when the disk is powered off. Once the HPA is removed, the hidden data contained in the area can be read. It is best to acquire data while the HPA is in place, than remove the HPA and retrieve the hidden data.

5.2.2 Chain of Custody

When acquiring evidence, a chain of custody must be established to ensure that the evidence and who has that evidence is known at all times. Additionally, the chain of custody also documents what actions were performed and by whom. Some important information must be gathered before imaging the machine:

- Name of individual seizing the drive

- Make of drive

- Model and Size of drive

- Serial Number

- Location of Seizure

- Time of Acquisition

- Method of Acquisition

- Exact commands types

- Other information

Some of this information may be difficult to obtain on a live system. Answer as much as possible and obtain the remaining information when the drive is powered down. Security of the original evidence is essential and must be maintained until the evidence is given to an evidence custodian or stored in a secure safe.

5.2.3 Mmls

If a drive has logical partitions, the mmls tool can be used to read the primary and extended partition tables. The tool will sort and list the partitions, as well as the locations of the disk not allocated to partitions. If mmls cannot determine the partition type, it must be specified. The information obtained by mmls is used to extract the partitions. The dd tool can be used to extract the partitions from the disk image using the following flags for each partition:

skip=*start*	Shows how many sections are to be skipped before copying starts
count=*length*	Defines how many sectors to copy
bs=*units*	Specifies the clock size

5.2.4 Mounting

The mount command will take a raw image and mount it to a specified directory. The contents of the image can then be read. The image must be in a recognizable file system.

Either of the commands below will mount a NTFS partition:

> # mount -t ntfs-3g -o loop,ro,show_sys_files/images /windowsforensics/ipcase_ntfs. img/mnt/hack/windows_mount

> # ntfs-3g -o loop,ro,show_sys_files/images /windowsforensics/ipcase_ntfs.img/mnt/ hack/windows_mount

The image should be examined on a safe system or a duplicate platform to boot. The system the image is on should be in read-only state. When a new partition is introduced in a Windows environment, the operating system will detect and mount the partition automatically. Or a duplicate image can be created in a similar hardware platform and booted to a mirrored computer to perform the analysis over the network.

5.3   Investigation and Analysis

5.3.1 Timeline Analysis

Timelines will identify the file access and modifications made to the victim system. Interpretation of the information is the most difficult of timeline analysis, whereas creating the timeline is the easiest activity. The process of timeline analysis involves gathering the file data and making a document of file activity that can be easily read by non-technical people.

To gather the required information, parse the file system to obtain the metadata information related to timelines, mainly MACtimes. The resulting file is known as the BODY file: it is gathered from the victim machine and stored on the analysis machine. From the analysis machine, the analysis is performed.

By creating the timeline, the investigator can see the system activity around the time of the incident, specifically viewing the files that were accessed, deleted, and modified, what tools were executed, and the patterns of activity. Even though there are methods and tools available to prevent access times from being stamped in the system, the commands required to initiate these processes are still logged.

Evidence on MACtimes is extremely sensitive: running a single command could rewrite the last access time on a file. Because of this, it is best to grab MACtimes data before any further commands run on the system. A documented timeline has seven columns:

- Time (with all same time entries grouped together)

- File size

- MACtimes

- Permissions and mode

- User and Group

- Metadata address

- File name

When the BODY file is first generated, it will have data on all files in the image. The data collected comes in three types:

- Allocated files - normal files

- Deleted file names - represents deleted files with existing name structures, and includes data such as times and permissions

- Unallocated inodes - identifies the files structures not in use by the system

The fls tool can be used to collect timeline information from the filename layer. The tool can output data in the mactime format using the -m <mount flag. The mounting point is required in the flag for cosmetic reasons. The syntax for the fls command is:

    # fls -r -m <mountpoint> <image/device>

A subset of the BODY file is used to create the timeline. The timeline will typically be created from the earliest data to the latest data and in a readable format. Password and group files can be used to replace numerical IDs. Similar items should be grouped together, such as user creation, password changes, compiled programs, and program installations. Particular attention should be given to noticeable hacker activity, such as newly created directories in odd places, large sized filed, and any writes into the system directories or /dev directory.

The mactime tool can take the data files from fls and create a timeline. The tool is a perl script. The timeline can created out of the entire time range or a restricted time range. The syntax of the command to use the tool is:

    # mactime <options> -b bodyfile <data-range>

5.3.2 Media Analysis

All files have a unique byte signature called a header. Some files can also have a footer. The headers for the same file will be identical even though they are on different file systems. The header is a key component to computer forensics. The value of the byte signature is called the magic number.

The contents of the data segment of a file can be examined by the 'file' tool. The tool will perform three sets of tests:

- File system tests

- Magic number tests

- Language tests

The tool allows easy identification of archives, shell scripts, and binaries for a large group of files.

5.3.3 String Searches

The srch_strings tool can be used to identify the exact location of a string on the drive, using the exact byte offset. The syntax of the tools is:

srch_strings [options] *filename*

The options available to srch_strings are:

-a	Grab all strings
-t {o,x,d}	Output offset in base 8, 10, or 16
-e l	Searching for little endian
-e b	Searching for big endian
-<num>	Allows a string of <num> length to be grabbed

The dirty word list created during responding to the incident can be used to search for the particular string in the evidence data. The best option to perform this search is to use the grep tool. It will perform binary analysis and string analysis. The strings of particular interest are:

- Email addresses

- URL addresses

- Usage statements

- Profanity

- k1dd13 sp34k

The syntax of the grep tool is:

> grep [options] *pattern filename*

5.3.4 Analysis Tools

The major set of tools used in forensic analysis is found in the Sleuth Kit provided as a free, open source suite at www.sleuthkit.org. Some tools are similar in function but used in different categories: 'cat' tools display data, 'state' tools display statistics, 'ls' tools list address details, and 'find' tools map between different layers. The tools are all based on Unix model of small specialized tools and code from The Coroner's Toolkit.

A total of 27 tools are found in the Sleuth Kit. Several tools are specifically designed for analysis of systems. The Sleuth Kit programs are divided into tools for:

- File system

- Data layer

- Metadata layer

- File name layer

- Journal layer

- Media Management layer

- Disk layer

How the tools are labeled explain what category they are in: respectively, fs, blk, l, f, j, mm, and disk.

Here is a list of the various tools:

- fsstat - displays the details about the file system partition

- blkcat - displays the contents of a disk block

- blkls - displays a list of contents for deleted disk blocks

- blkcalc - displays maps between dd images and blkls results

- blkstat - displays the list of statistics related to specific disk blocks

- ils - displays inode details

- istat - displays specific inode information

- icat - displays contents of blocks allocated to an inode

- ifind - displays the inode allocated to a block

- fls - displays file and directory entries in a directory inode

- ffind - displays the file which has allocated by an inode in an image

- jls - displays the list of entries in a file system journal

- jcat - displays the contents of a clock in a file system journal

- mmls - displays the list of partitions or disk slices

- mmstat - displays partition type information

- disk_stat - displays information on ATA hard disk size

- disk_sreset - removes an HPA

5.4   Automated Toolkits

5.4.1 Sorter Tool

The sorter tool is a perl script found in the Sleuth Kit. It will run the fls tool to obtain a list of file paths and then will run icat on each file. The data obtained from is forwarded to the file command and the content identified. The results are either noted or saved in a directory. Hash lookups can be performed.

Specific flags can be used to get particular results:

-e	Displays extension mismatches only
-s	Saves data to category directories
-h	Used with -s option to produce thumbnails
-d	Specifies the directory for saving information
-c	Specifies the configuration file
-m	Specifies the mount point
-E	Displays category indexing only
-l	Lists the details to STDOUT only

5.4.2 Hash Comparisons

Hash databases are used to detect "known good" or "known bad" files. The entries in the database consist of MD5 or SHA-1 hashes. The Sleuth Kit provides the hfind tool to lookup files in these databases. The output of the tool is an idx file corresponding to the database. The syntax of the hfind tool command is:

hfind -I <index_type> <hash_database_file>

Well known databases will support md5sum, National Software Reference Library (NSRL), and Hashkeeper formats. Hash databases will contain known good files, known bad files or both. Known good files are confirmed as benign and will not impact the case. Files that are known to be good can be eliminated from the image. Known bad files are always of interest in every case. These files should be highlighted from the evidence image.

To create a list of known files, use md5deep. The command will recursively go through the file system to calculate MD5 hashes. SHA-1, SHA-256, Tiger or Whirlpool hashes can be performed with the -deep suffix. The command will look at all the files and directories on the system and create a hash output file with the results of md5sum on every file.

The National Software Reference Library (NSRL) is a part of the National Institute Science and Technology (NIST) which provides a collection of file hash values, specifically known good files pertaining to operating systems and applications.

The sorter tool can also perform hash comparisons on known good and known bad files. Before the sorter tool can work properly, the databases must be indexed using the hfind tool. The following options to the hfind tool will determine if sorting is performed on bad files or good files:

-a	Alert Hash list (bad files)
-x	Exclude Hash List (good files)
-n	NSR Database (good files)

A good preparation for any incident is to hash all files on a system before an incident occurs. This ensures that a list of hashes is available to the investigator on all 'good' files.

5.4.3 Fuzzy Hashing

Typical hash algorithms will perform actions on the entire file. However, what happens when similar files are encountered, such as altered documents or partial files? Some hash programs can hash and compare similar parts of a file. Called fuzzy hashing or piecewise hashing, this process will divide a file into smaller pieces and examine those smaller pieces. The hashing algorithms used are called context triggered piecewise hashing (CTPH).

With CTPH, the ssdeep tool is used to compare files that are similar, but different. The syntax for the ssdeep tool is:

ssdeep -m file_of_hashes [options] FILES

Some of the options available to the ssdeep tool are:

-m file of hashes	Loads the file of hashes for comparisons
-r	Enables recursive mode
-p	Enables pretty matching mode
-d	Enables directory mode
-b	Strips the leading directory information
-l	Displays relative file path

5.4.4 Autopsy Forensic Browser

The Autopsy Forensic Browser is a graphical interface alternative to the command line tools already discussed. It provides an interface to the Sleuth Kit tools and other standard tools for Unix. The browser is really an HTML server which can execute the commands required to use the tools from the Sleuth Kit, parse the output, and generate HTML output to be seen from any browser.

5.5 Windows Forensics – Incident Response

5.5.1 Windows Forensic Toolkit

The Windows Forensic Toolkit (WFT) provides automated evidence collection and incident response on a Windows system. It is a batch processing shell capable of running other security tools. HTML reports can be produced by the toolkit for forensic investigations. The toolkit is designed to provide information which is useful in court proceedings but can also be used by the average user. Its logging of toolkit activities along with MD5 checksums makes the process reliable for legal investigations.

WFT is designed to be run from a CD. Because of this, the CD must be prepared. Of particular interest is ensuring all executables and DLLs (binaries) for the forensic tools are on the CD and the configuration file must be customized with the appropriate tools and MD5. The first tool always run in a forensic situation is the cmd.exe utility.

Below are some uses of the WFT program:

- To output usage instructions:

    - wft [-h] [-help] [-?] [-usage]

- To output MD5 checksums for FILE filename:

    - wft [-md5 filename]

- To execute WFT:

    - wft [-cfg cfgfile] [-dst destination] [-shell cmdshell] [-noslow] [-nowrite] [--noreport]

In the last command, the options included provide the following capabilities:

-cfg cfgfile	Will use the cfgfile to determine which tools to run
-dst destination	Defines the path which reports will be written to
-shell cmdshell	Redefines the shell references from cmd.exe to cmdshell
-noslow	Will not run slow executables in cfgfile
-nowrite	Will not run executables that write to source machine
-noreport	Will not create HTML reports

Output from WFT can consists of a combination of:

- Memory images

- System information

- Process information

- Network information

- File system and Registry information

Information about the system environment is typically provided by the psinfo tool. Psinfo is a command-line tool to provide information on the local or remote Windows NT/2000 systems, such as:

- Installation type

- Kernel build

- System install date

- Registered owner and organization

- Number of processors

- Processor type

- Physical memory size

The pslist tool will provide information for all processes currently running on the local system. The information included on each process is:

- Time of execution

- Time length the process has executed in kernel mode and user mode

- Amount of physical memory allocated to the process

For network information, the fport tool will gather information on open ports and sockets, TCP and UDP ports, and map the ports to the application which own them. The tool will also determine which applications are listening on network connections. Use the netstat tool to confirm findings or obtain information not available through fport. Using switches, the results from fport can be sorted by application, process ID, application path, or by port.

Once the information on memory image, system, processes, network, and password have been collected, the disk image can be collected.

5.5.2 Windows Forensics - Media Analysis

In Windows, media analysis includes:

- Registry Analysis

- UserAssist Keys

- Restore Point Analysis

- Shadow Copy Volume Analysis

- Windows Prefetch

- Review of Pertinent Files

- Internet Explorer History Files

- Thumbs.db and Thumbsache

- Recycle Bin (XP and Vista)

5.5.3 Registry Analysis

The system's vital configuration data on hardware, software, and system components are stored in the registry. These are data files which can tell the investigator with software has been installed, the configuration of the system, the most recently used files, and the programs that are executed at startup. The registry is viewed and manipulated using 'regedt32'.

Four root keys exist in the registry:

- HKEY_CLASSES_ROOT

- HKEY_CURRENT_USER

- HKEY_LOCAL_MACHINE

- HKEY_USERS

An investigator can access the registry on a live system or when it is off line. If accessing off line, knowledge of the registries location is required: the majority of registry files are in \%WINDIR%\system32\config directory. All system setup, startup files, machine configuration, and default files exist in the HKEY_LOCAL_MACHINE. The registry hives are:

- SAM - stores information on all local user accounts and groups.

- SECURITY - stores security information used by the SAM and operating system.

- SOFTWARE - stores data for all application settings, including Windows programs and products.

- SYSTEM - stores data on the hardware and service configuration, including a list of raw device names for volumes and drives.

- NTUSER.DAT - stores configuration and environment settings for individual users.

The registry has a section for each user in the NTUSER.DAT. With the information contained in the section, each user can be profiled. Specific information provided includes:

- Last login

- Last failed login

- Logon count

- Password policy

- Search history

- Typed URLs

- Last Commands executed

- Last files saved

- Application execution history

When investigating systems with multiple users, the user's Security Identifier (SID) can be tracked instead of the username.

The regtime.pl tool can be used to create a timeline of the registry. It does this by parsing the registry and pulling all the last write times from every key. The last updates in the registry can be compared to the timeline for the file system. The syntax for the tool command is:

    # perl regtime.pl -m <HIVETYPE> -r <HIVEFILE> bodyfile

5.5.4 Restore Point Forensics

A system will generate a restore point every 24 hours the system is on. The purpose of a restore point is to enable a user to restore the system to a previous date. They are found on Windows XP and Windows ME machines. Included in the XP Restore Point are:

- Registry files

- Creation Times

- Change Log

- Data and Files

A restore point number contains one or more change logs which map files stored in the restore point. The restore point times are stored in the rp.log along with the name of each restore point. The tool will take the 64-bit Windows time and extract the last 8-bits. This is the creation time for the restore point.

5.5.5 Shadow Forensics

Windows Vista and Windows 7 systems provide the Volume Shadow Copy Service (VSS). Commonly called the shadow copy, a person can roll back a file, a folder, or the entire file system to a previous restoration point. When a file or folder is changed or deleted, the shadow copy allows a user to revert the file to any previous version, restore the file, or make a copy of the previous version. Specifically, the function creates a cluster by cluster backup of system and file information. A snapshot of the system is taken once a day.

Only 15% of the disk space is allocated to maintain any shadow copies; therefore, the number of copies available to an investigator depends on the size of the copies. A list of existing volumes can be determined by executing the tool vssadmin, using the syntax:

      C:\> vssadmin list shadows /for=C:

If examining the contents of a specific volume, the name of the shadow copy volume is the name of the volume. If examining volumes from another shadow copy enabled machine, the originating machine name is important. The system time of the volume's creation time will defined when the volume was created.

The dd.exe tool can be used to image a shadow volume. The resulting image will be full logical image from the VSS enabled machine.

5.5.6 Windows Prefetch

The Windows prefetch is a directory containing files designed to improve the efficiency of the system. Most of the files are pre-loaded critical sections of applications. By having the operating system load key data and code into memory before it is required, the user has this information already available when they want to execute application, namely those applications they use most often. The prefetch directory is filled with data when the application is executed: therefore it is best to grab the contents of the directory before performing any incident response. The Cache Manager is used to monitor all files and directories referenced by individual applications and processes.

A prefetch file can be recognized by its naming convention: the executable's name followed by a hex-based representation of the hash of the file path and a .pf extension. Within the file is information on the number of times the application has been executed, the original path of the execution, and the last time the application was executed.

Found in XP and Vista systems, the prefetch feature is limited to 128 files. (In Vista, prefetch is known as Superfetch). The layout.ini file contains the files and directories used by the prefetch process. The file is written to after the operating system examines the contents of .pf files, which is done on a regular basis. The layout.ini is also used by the Disk Defragmenter to relocate all the directories and files to contiguous areas.

5.5.7 E-mail Forensics

Many computer crimes involve e-mail communications or attacks. Three situations are often faced by investigators when dealing with e-mail:

- E-mail files stored locally on a machine in *.pst files.

- E-mail files stored on an Exchange or Lotus Notes server.

- E-mail accounts through free services.

With locally stored e-mail files, a search on the hard drive can be conducted to identify where the .pst files are. They can be copied and imported to an Outlook application offline. Every email received from location to location is stamped with MTA information in its header. This stamping is performed by the SMTP gateway and will show the IP address from the originating system, even if the e-mail address has been spoofed. MTA, or Message Transfer Agents, are used to exchange e-mail using SMTP on port 25.

When dealing with e-mail files on Exchange or Lotus Notes servers, it is best to obtain the backups for the servers. Also on the server is information on the account and log files. The .pst mailboxes of the subject can be exported by the e-mail administrator.

When users are using a free service, acquisition of e-mail data requires working with authorities to subpoena the information from the service provider. Investigations of e-mail messages are extremely vital when determine who sent a message (threat) or in determining the accurate identity of a sender.

5.5.8 Thumbnail Forensics

The Thumbs database (Thumbs.db) is a hidden file in directories which have pictures stored within. The pictures or images are cataloged and a copy of the picture stored as a thumbnail even when the pictures are deleted. The directory must be able to view the files in thumbnail or filmstrip modes.

In Vista, the Thumbs.db does not exist. Instead, the data resides in a single directory for each user of the machine. The directory is called a thumbcache: is location is C:\Users\<username>\AppData\Local\Microsoft\Windows\Explorer. Thumbnails can come in 4 sizes: small (32 bit), medium (96 bit), large (256 bit) and extra large (1024 bits). A different thumbcache exists for each size.

5.6   Application Footprinting

Eventually, an investigator will arrive at a point where forensic data is sought in individual programs or devices. Application footprinting examines the information of a program with the operating system. Of interest is if the application was executed and any trace evidence that may exist even when the application has been deleted. Each application will interact with the system in a specific way, particularly concerning file access, registry keys, file creation and modification. Every application will have installation files, log files, temporary files, and registry keys.

Four tools are required to analyze the application footprint:

- HELIX bootable CDROM

- VMWare Image

- Active Registry Monitor

- Timeline Analysis

5.6.1 Active Registry Monitor

The Active Registry Monitor (ARM) is designed to analyze changes mede to the Windows registry. This is done by taking snapshots of the registry and maintaining them in a browsable database. Two snapshots can be compared and a list of keys and data obtained which have been added, deleted, or modified.

5.6.2 Process of Application Footprinting

The steps for performing application footprinting are:

1. Create a baseline image and image snapshot.

2. Use ARM to create an initial registry snapshot and save to disk.

3. Boot from the HELIX CD and obtain a timeline using the fls, ils, and mactime tools.

4. Plug in U3 USB Device.

5. Take another Registry Snapshot and use "Compare Here" option to identify new and modified keys.

6. Identify a USB device.

7. Identify the setupapi.dev.log (setupapi.log in Vista).

8. Acquire data from user's browser.

9. Identify what artifacts exist after using a file wiper (easily performed using the Digital File Shredder Pro).

10. DFSP.exe will show up in Prefetch.

11. A directory renamed UUUUUUUUU is downloaded.

12. MainApp2.ico is created on the machine.

13. Remove the U3 USB device.

6 Practice Exam

6.1 Refresher "Warm up Questions"

The following multiple-choice questions are a refresher.

Question 1

Which of the following evidence should be gathered first in an investigation?

    A.   Volatile data on the system

    B.   System images

    C.   Log data, IDS, and interviews

    D.   Network connections

Question 2

Which of the following is an essential principle for an investigator?

    A.   Minimize impact of incident

    B.   Right everything down

    C.   Find source of the incident

    D.   All of the above

Question 3

What is the purpose of the verification step in the Forensic Investigation Methodology?

    A.   Ensure an incident has occurred.

    B.   Ensure the analysis was performed correctly.

    C.   Ensure all the evidence has been collected.

    D.   Verify results with authorities.

Question 4

What is the length of each entry in the partition table?

    A.   1 bytes

    B.   8 bytes

    C.   16 bytes

    D.   4 bits

Question 5

What is basic unit structure of the metadata layer?

    A.   Data

    B.   Inodes

    C.   Bytes

    D.   Blocks

Question 6

Which of the following computer crime offenses are not covered by the Computer Fraud and Abuse Act?

    A.   Computer attack resulting in losses of $4000.

    B.   Turning off environmental systems in facility.

    C.   Breaking into a TSA computer.

    D.   Accessing and changing medical prescriptions

Question 7

What is the primary legislation for computer crimes in the European Union?

A.   Computer Misuse Act of 1990

B.   Data Retention Directive

C.   Strafgesetzbuch

D.   Data Protection Directive

Question 8

What characteristics should an investigative report have?

A.   Lots of technical jargon to show competency

B.   Conclusions found through sound methods

C.   Analysis which is specific to prosecuting attackers

D.   Documented work which will only lead to prosecution

Question 9

Which of the following statements about honeypots is not true?

A.   All persons who access the honeypot are trespassers.

B.   The use of honeypots has not been tested legally.

C.   Prior consent of a party is not required.

D.   Only law enforcement can use honeypots to entrap attackers.

Question 10

Which of the following is not a benefit of hashing?

    A.   Authentication

    B.   Tampering

    C.   Law versus Science

    D.   Expert Witnessing

Question 11

What are honeypots?

    A.   Illegal configurations to attract attackers

    B.   Entrapment configurations used after detecting an intrusion

    C.   Non-production servers which look like production servers

    D.   All of the above

Question 12

The integrity of evidence is preserved through what technique?

    A.   Access Control

    B.   Hash functions

    C.   Secure storage

    D.   Chain of Custody

Question 13

Which U.S. statute is specifically focused on the information related to a communications rather than the content of the information?

    A.   Pen/Trap Statue

    B.   ECPA

    C.   Wiretap Act

    D.   Computer Fraud and Abuse Act

Question 14

Which directory of a Linux file system stores configuration items?

    A.   /bin

    B.   /etc

    C.   /proc

    D.   /dev

Question 15

Which layer of a file system contains information on the structure of the file system?

    A.   File system

    B.   Physical

    C.   File name

    D.   Metadata

Question 16

For x86-based systems, what is the byte address of the third partition?

    A.   446

    B.   462

    C.   478

    D.   494

Question 17

Which of the following steps of the Forensic Investigation Methodology is part of the incident response portion of the investigation?

    A.   Media Analysis

    B.   System Description

    C.   Data Recovery

    D.   Timeline Analysis

Question 18

What is the purpose of a key word list?

    A.   To perform low level searches on the hard drive

    B.   To provide indexing to evidence data

    C.   To identify communication points with investigators

    D.   All of the above

Question 19

In which of the following places is data the least volatile?

    A.   CD-ROM disk

    B.   RAM memory

    C.   Hard drives

    D.   Virtual memory

Question 20

What Mac file system format can be analyzed by the SIFT Forensic Workstation?

    A.   VFAT

    B.   HFS

    C.   EXT2/3

    D.   UFS

Question 21

Which of the following is a major focus for evidence gathering techniques?

    A.   Minimizing downtime

    B.   Avoiding data changes

    C.   Minimizing loss of data

    D.   All of the above

Question 22

SYN attacks are a form of what type of threat?

    A.   Buffer overflows

    B.   Spoofing

    C.   Denial of service

    D.   Backdoor

Question 23

The numerical expression, 1xF3, is in what format?

    A.   Hexadecimal

    B.   Base 10

    C.   Binary

    D.   Base 8

Question 24

Which of the following data in the partition entry is used by forensic tools?

    A.   Logical start of the partition

    B.   Length of partitions

    C.   Partition type

    D.   All of the above

Question 25

In Linux, what is a superblock?

      A.   A listing of all the allocated space on the disk.

      B.   A listing of all the free space on the disk.

      C.   Multiple blocks joined and used for a large file

      D.   Multiple blocks joined and used for an application

Question 26

Which of the following is not a category of stored electronic communications covered by the Electronic Communications Privacy Act?

      A.   Stored device information

      B.   Stored content of communications

      C.   Subscriber and billing information

      D.   Stored communications associated data

Question 27

Which of the following principles of data protection is not defined in the EU Data Protection Directive?

      A.   Foreign Transfer

      B.   Notice and Consent

      C.   Authentication

      D.   Security of Processing

Question 28

When presenting legal evidence, what is not a basic rule?

    A.   Unaltered

    B.   Relatedness

    C.   Best Evidence

    D.   Authentication

Question 29

What is not an item that an investigator must bring to an incident?

    A.   CAT5 cable

    B.   Small hub

    C.   Drive adapters for SATA/IDE/SCSI

    D.   Straightforward cable

Question 30

Which of the following is not a root key in the Windows registry?

    A.   HKEY_CLASSES_ROOT

    B.   HKEY_CURRENT_USER

    C.   HKEY_REMOTE_MACHINE

    D.   HKEY_USERS

Question 31

Which of the following tools should be part of the incident response bootable disc should be available for Windows support?

    A.   cmd.exe

    B.   netstat

    C.   ifconfig

    D.   lsof

Question 32

Which of the following is a characteristic of a lay witness?

    A.   Specialized knowledge

    B.   No personal experience of issue

    C.   Opinions based on fact

    D.   Opinions based on perception

Question 33

What type of evidence is used to suggest innocence?

    A.   Inculpatory

    B.   Exculpatory

    C.   Consensual

    D.   Explicit

Question 34

Which of the following exceptions listed in the United States Wiretap Act allow communications to be intercepted if the system is being used as a pass-through system?

A. Computer Trespasser Exception

B. Provider Exception

C. Consent of a Party Exception

D. Any of the above

Question 35

Which of the following Unix file types are really aliases to other files?

A. Directories

B. Named pipes

C. Symbolic links

D. Named sockets

Question 36

Which of the following file systems measures data units in terms of clusters?

A. FFS

B. NTFS

C. EXT2FS

D. All of the above

Question 37

What is the binary representation of the number 54?

    A.   00110110

    B.   36

    C.   01101100

    D.   63

Question 38

Phishing is what type of attack?

    A.   Buffer Overflow

    B.   Denial of Service

    C.   Tapping

    D.   Masquerading

Question 39

What is the smallest piece of evidence usable in computer forensics?

    A.   1 byte

    B.   4 bytes

    C.   1 bit

    D.   4 bits

Question 40

What is the best description of computer forensics?

      A.   The collection of volatile and non-volatile data.

      B.   The analysis of data for the purpose of identifying and resolving incidents.

      C.   A process for gathering and analyzing data free from distortion or bias.

      D.   The process for finding and prosecuting violators of computer protection laws.

7   Answer Guide

7.1   Answers to Questions

Question 1

Answer: D

Reasoning: The first set of data gathered in an investigation should be any information on network connections. This is performed before the system is disconnected and system information is collected.

Question 2

Answer: B

Reasoning: The four essential principles of forensic investigations are minimize data loss, right everything down, analyze all collected data, and report findings.

Question 3

Answer: A

Reasoning: The verification step is the first step of the Forensic Investigation Methodology and confirms the existence of an incident.

Question 4

Answer: C

Reasoning: Each entry in the partition tables is exactly 16 bytes long.

Question 5

Answer: B

Reasoning: The metadata layer is comprised of inodes, either allocated or unallocated.

Question 6

Answer: A

Reasoning: A violation of the act is based on a loss of at least $5000 to one of more persons over a year, modification or impairment of medical examinations, diagnosis and treatment, or care, physical injury to a person, threat to public health or safety, or damage to a computer system used by or for the government. The loss of $4000 is not covered by the Computer Fraud and Abuse Act.

Question 7

Answer: D

Reasoning: The Data Protection Directive was passed by the European Union and requires all Member States to pass national laws supporting the directive. The Computer Misuse Act of 1990 and the Strafgesetzbuch are national laws supporting the directive from the United Kingdom and Germany respectively.

Question 8

Answer: B

Reasoning: The best reports minimize the technical jargon, provide conclusions from sound methods, provide results that are repeated and reliable, thorough and unbiased analysis, and documented work which can be replicated.

Question 9

Answer: C

Reasoning: Honeypots have not been tested legally in a court of law; however a few exceptions from legislation such as the Wiretap Act can ensure that honeypots are consistent with legal concerns. Entrapment is only a concern when honeypots are implemented by law enforcement. Honeypots are either access by persons who are unauthorized or by persons who have given consent to monitoring. Prior content is one of the exceptions to provide legal stance to honeypots.

Question 10

Answer: A

Reasoning: Hashing ensures the integrity of the evidence and is not required to admit evidence. The benefits of hashing to evidence are it provides confidence in expert witnesses, ensures the evidence is not tampered with, and clarifies the science versus the law.

Question 11

Answer: C

Reasoning: Honeypots are non-production servers which act as production servers to attract attackers. They are not illegal if they fulfill a number of guidelines related to intent, configuration, and activity. They are generally implemented to detect intrusions, but may be implemented after intrusion is suspected to obtain more information.

Question 12

Answer: D

Reasoning: Chain of Custody is a technique to ensure the integrity of evidence from acquisition to prosecution.

Question 13

Answer: A

Reasoning: The Pen Registers and Trap and Trace Device statute, or Pen/Trap Statute, applies to header information of a communication and not the content of the communication, specifically to allow providers to capture the initiation and completion of communications.

Question 14

Answer: B

Reasoning: The /etc directory stores configuration items in the Linux file system.

Question 15

Answer: D

Reasoning: The Metadata layer provides information on the structure of the file system.

Question 16

Answer: C

Reasoning: The byte address for x86-based systems on the hard drive is byte 478 in the first 512 byte sector.

Question 17

Answer: B

Reasoning: Incident Response encompasses three of the eight steps of the Forensic Investigation Methodology: Verification, System Description, and Evidence Acquisition.

Question 18

Answer: A

Reasoning: Key word lists are created for each investigation to identify how to perform low level searches on the hard drive or other media.

Question 19

Answer: C

Reasoning: Data found on hard drive disks is considered non-volatile, or the least volatile of data. Data found on CD-ROM or floppy disk would be the a little more volatile, followed by RAM and virtual memory.

Question 20

Answer: B

Reasoning: The SIFT Forensic Workstation can be used to analyze several files systems on different operating systems: for Windows - MSDOS, FAT, VFAT, NTFS; Mac – HFS; Solaris – UFS; Linux – EXT2/3.

Question 21

Answer: D

Reasoning: The techniques for evidence gathering focus on minimizing data loss, avoiding changes to system data, recovering service and data, and minimizing downtime.

Question 22

Answer: C

Reasoning: SYN attacks are a form of Denial of Service attack, where the number of open-ended session requests is overwhelming enough to prevent the service to be available authorized personnel.

Question 23

Answer: A

Reasoning: Hexadecimal is a base 16 system where numbers are represented with the numbers 0-9 and characters A-F.

Question 24

Answer: D

Reasoning: The three primary areas of the partition entry used by forensic tools are the partition type, logical start of the partition, and the length of partitions in sectors.

Question 25

Answer: B

Reasoning: The superblock is a listing of all the free space on the disk.

Question 26

Answer: A

Reasoning: The covered categories of the Electronic Communications Privacy Act are the stored content of communications, stored communications associated data, and subscriber and billing information.

Question 27

Answer: C

Reasoning: The key principles of data protection law are Notice and Consent, Security of Processing, Access, and Foreign Transfer.

Question 28

Answer: B

Reasoning: The following rules are for legal evidence: relevance, authentication, unaltered, and best evidence.

Question 29

Answer: D

Reasoning: An investigator should bring a package of equipment to initiate the investigation, including a small hub or switch, CAT5 cable, cross-over cable, incident response disk, drive adapter for SATA/IDE/SCSI, and large capacity portable drive.

Question 30

Answer: C

Reasoning: Four root keys are part of the Windows registry:

HKEY_CLASSES_ROOT

HKEY_CURRENT_USER

HKEY_REMOTE_MACHINE

HKEY_USERS

Question 31

Answer: A

Reasoning: Windows tools should include cmd.exe and the NT Resource Kit.

Question 32

Answer: D

Reasoning: The characteristics of a lay witness involve personal knowledge of the issue, no specialized knowledge, and opinion based on perception.

Question 33

Answer: B

Reasoning: Exculpatory data is acquired to suggest innocence.

Question 34

Answer: A

Reasoning: The Computer Trespasser Exception allows law enforcement to intercept communications if the trespasser is using the system as a pass-through to attack other systems.

Question 35

Answer: C

Reasoning: Symbolic links are aliases to other files in the Unix file system.

Question 36

Answer: B

Reasoning: The FAT and NTFS file systems define data units in terms of clusters, while FFS and EXT2FS file systems define data units in terms of blocks.

Question 37

Answer: A

Reasoning: The binary expression for 54 is 0011011. The hexadecimal expression is 36.

Question 38

Answer: D

Reasoning: Phishing is a form of masquerading where Internet users are redirected from valid websites to malicious sites.

Question 39

Answer: B

Reasoning: The smallest piece of data available to be used in computer forensics is 4 bytes which is two octets of an IP address.

Question 40

Answer: C

Reasoning: The best description for computer forensics is as a process for gathering and analyzing data free from distortion or bias. The data collected can be volatile or non-volatile. The analysis performed can be used to identify and resolve incidents. The result of the investigation can result in the prosecution of individuals committing computer crimes.

8   References

Security 508 Computer Forensics Investigation and Response: Forensic and Investigative Essentials. The SANS Institute:2009.

Security 508 Computer Forensics Investigation and Response: Forensic Methodology Illustrated. The SANS Institute:2009.

Security 508 Computer Forensics Investigation and Response: Windows Forensics. The SANS Institute:2009.

Security 508 Computer Forensics Investigation and Response: Computer Investigative Law for Forensic Analysts. The SANS Institute:2009.

Security 508 Computer Forensics Investigation and Response: Advanced Forensics and the Forensic Challenge. The SANS Institute:2009.

GIAC information: www.giac.com

Websites

www.artofservice.com.au

www.theartofservice.org

www.theartofservice.com

9   Index

A

B

bytes   14, 26-31, 37, 40, 72, 90, 101, 103, 106, 111

C

cable   65, 67, 98, 109

CD-ROM   35, 65, 107

chain   19, 59, 61

Chain of Custody   6-7, 59, 73, 92, 105

Change Log   85

characters   18, 37, 108

clusters   21-2, 28-30, 36-8, 40-1, 85, 100, 110

command   33-5, 48, 67-8, 71, 74-5, 78-80

communication content   49, 52

communications   16, 19-20, 42, 44, 49-52, 58, 62-4, 93, 97, 100, 106, 108, 110

companies   3, 22, 53, 72

computer   11, 20-1, 26, 48, 50, 52-3, 63, 72, 74, 104

computer crimes   46, 55, 86, 91

computer forensics   1, 4, 9, 13-14, 76, 101-2, 111

Computer Fraud and Abuse Act   6, 46, 48, 90, 93

Computer Misuse Act   6, 52, 91, 104

computer trespasser exception   50, 63, 100, 110

confidentiality   15, 45, 51-2

consent   49-51, 56, 58, 63, 97, 100, 105, 108

copy   14-15, 31, 59, 68-71, 73, 85, 87

court   25, 55, 59-61, 68, 105

custody   6-7, 59, 73, 92, 105

D

E

information 13-14, 16-17, 19-25, 29, 31-2, 36-8, 43-5, 47-53, 58-9, 67, 73-4, 81-2, 84, 86-7, 93, 103

inodes 30-3, 78, 90, 104

integrity 14-15, 48, 51-2, 59, 66-8, 72, 105

interception 47, 50, 62-4

Internet 22, 25, 42

intrusions 46, 92, 105

investigative reports 6, 60, 91

investigators 5, 12-15, 25, 33, 42, 44-5, 60, 63, 65, 68-70, 74, 80, 83-7, 89, 94, 98

IP 19, 23, 26

K

keys 18-20, 60, 84, 87-8

L

law enforcement 5, 44-5, 48-50, 58, 60, 62-3, 69, 91, 110

laws 9-10, 42, 46-7, 52, 68, 92, 105

layers 20, 29-30, 77, 93

legal process 49-50, 58

legislation 48, 55, 105

liability 3, 56, 62

Linux 12, 31, 35, 69, 72, 97, 107

Linux File System 5, 34, 106

Linux systems 31, 33, 35, 71-2

list 14, 18, 30-2, 42, 68, 73, 77-80, 84-5, 88

live systems 14, 65-6, 69, 73, 84

location 15, 23, 25, 27, 38, 53, 59, 73, 86-7

logging 33, 58, 81

losses 3, 48, 57, 90, 104

M

machine 35, 58, 73-4, 83-8, 98

MACtimes 40, 74-5

management 17, 21, 32-3, 43-4, 60

masquerading 19, 101, 111

md5 71, 79, 81

media 14-15, 21, 23, 67, 69, 107

media analysis 7, 14, 24-5, 76, 83, 94

Member States 52, 54-7, 104

memory 16-19, 21, 67-8, 86

metadata 29-30, 70, 93

metadata layer 5, 30, 32-3, 40-1, 77, 90, 104, 106

mmls 7, 73, 78

mobile code 4, 15, 17

modification 25, 48, 53, 74, 87, 104

monitoring 50, 52, 62-3, 105

mount 29, 35, 66, 74

Verification   24, 66, 106

victims   23, 42-4, 48, 62

Vista   36, 83, 86-8

volatile   13, 42, 70, 102, 107, 111

volatile data   13, 67, 89

volume   37-8, 40-1, 84-5

vulnerabilities   17, 21-3, 45-6

W

Windows   12, 30, 36-7, 66, 68-9, 71-2, 74, 83, 87-8, 107

Windows Forensics   7, 81, 83, 112

Windows Prefetch   8, 83, 86

wire   47, 51, 64

Wiretap Act   50, 52, 62-3, 93, 105

witness   59-61, 99, 109

workstation   12, 24, 67, 70